A DEVOTIONAL JOURNAL

122

Love Letters

from the

Throne of Grace

A DEVOTIONAL JOURNAL

122
Love Letters
from the
Throne of Grace

122 love letters filled with Scripture references, powerful prayers, and exercises that will draw you into deeper intimacy with your Heavenly Daddy, Jesus, and Holy Spirit.

NICHOLE MARBACH

CSA
PUBLISHING

Published by CSA Publishing
A department of Christian Services Association
P.O. Box 1017
Maricopa, Arizona 85139
Unites States of America
www.XPpublishing.com

ISBN 978-1-936101-41-2

CSA
PUBLISHING

ENDORSEMENTS

"In the book, **122 LOVE LETTERS from the Throne of Grace,** Nichole brings out the very heart of God to the people. She ushers in a voice that speaks to the very spirit of humanity and brings an awakening and a fire to the embers buried deep inside. This devotional will help bring healing to the broken-hearted and will restore faith back to those who have been in hopelessness. I highly recommend Nichole and her work in the Kingdom of God. She is a jewel to the Father."

Dr. Jeremy Lopez
Founder of Identity Network
www.identitynetwork.net

"Nichole's new devotional book is filled with beautiful revelation about God's love and goodness. I know that these pages will bless you and fill your heart with peace as you read and meditate upon His Word."

Joshua Mills
President, The Intensified Glory Institute®
Palm Springs, California/Langley, British Columbia
www.IntensifiedGlory.com

"I have found Nichole's daily devotional to be heartfelt, transparent and powerful. Her simple, intimate sharing style speaks right into the heart and soul of those who desire to know the heartbeat of their Heavenly Father. I recommend this book to anyone from the most broken, to the most mature. This book will help anyone, from all walks of life, in all levels of relationship with God to grow closer in intimacy with Him."

XP Pastor Mark Kuntz
www.greaterworkshealing.com

"Nichole's daily devotional is an invitation to come as a child and step into the tender, unfailing, relentless love of God. To all who come, He will meet you as you read these words."

Lisa Lato
Come and Receive Ministries
www.comeandreceive.com

"Nichole's devotional radiates hope that love can change a soul and inspire abundant living. The overwhelming love of the Father has transformed Nichole's life and can transform yours, too. Welcome to the love of Abba, our Heavenly Daddy. These devotions testify to the river of love flowing from His throne to our hearts. His love knows no bounds!"

Pastor Fred and Ingrid De Jong
CenterPointe Church
www.cpwired.org

"**122 LOVE LETTERS from the Throne of Grace** reveals the character of God and the depth of His unconditional love for all creation. This book can bring life, encouragement, and spiritual understanding to the reader. Nichole, may God's blessings rest upon this tremendous work and those who read it because of your obedience and His great love."

Bonny J. San Hamel
Servant of the Most High God

"Nichole's new book, '**122 LOVE LETTERS from the Throne of Grace**' is a wonderful devotional book. Nichole writes from such a personal place out of her walk with her Heavenly Father. God is a personal God and her letters show his heart and kindness to His children. I encourage you to read these letters every morning and then think upon your Heavenly Father all day long for He is truly thinking of you."

Julie Meyer
International House Of Prayer - KC
www.juliemeyer.com

"Knowing God's tender love for you is vital. '**122 LOVE LETTERS from the Throne of Grace**' by Nichole Marbach will introduce you to deeper realms of His love and grace. Expect encounter!"

Patricia King
xpmedia.com

"I so recommend this book, **122 LOVE LETTERS from the Throne of Grace**. It was truly birthed from the Throne Room of God." I met Nichole at a Glory School and have gotten to know her personally. She is the real deal! I suggest anyone who wishes to understand their destiny to get this book."

Theresa Phillips
Chicago Prophetic Voice
www.chicagopropheticvoice.net

ACKNOWLEDGEMENTS

I would like to express my deepest appreciation to my Lord and Savior, Jesus Christ, for enduring the cross, buying me back, becoming my sin, purchasing my entire inheritance, and setting me completely free from all sickness and bondage. Jesus, You are and will always be Lord of my life. Your love has truly set me free to live.

I am eternally grateful for my wonderful husband, Claude, for standing by me in my darkest hour. He showed me the love of Christ, and I thank him with all of my heart. I am so grateful to our Heavenly Daddy that we are now reaping the blessings of sticking together for better or for worse. I would also like to thank my three beautiful children, Tiphanie, Lexy, and Lucas for supporting me during the process of writing this book. You are all precious to me, and I love you with all of my heart.

I would especially like to thank my close friend and ministry partner, Lisa Lato, for how she has helped me grow spiritually. Lisa has helped me to understand in a deeper way the blessings of the cross and Christ's love for me. I am so grateful for all the laughter and joy we have shared together and know there will be many more times. Your mentoring, wisdom, honesty, and friendship continue to be a huge gift in my life. I know Heavenly Father put us together for "such a time as this." Thank you for being such a faithful, loyal, loving friend.

I would like to thank Ernie and Diana Welchel of Glory Crown Ministries. The Lord has used you to equip me to do the works of the Kingdom and to help me step out in faith in the prophetic. Your desire to see broken, hurting people healed and set free by Jesus has touched my heart in a deep way. Thank you for being in my life and for continuing to help me go higher spiritually. You are a blessing to me and the entire Body of Christ.

Special thanks from my heart to Mark and Cathy Kuntz, my XP Pastors, for their continued support of me writing these love letters. Christ's love shines through both of them, and they are a huge blessing to me and to many others. Thank you for your unconditional love and acceptance and encouragement to get these devotionals out to the Body of Christ, and for helping me to walk into my destiny. I am very grateful to have you in my life.

I would also like to thank Fred and Ingrid De Jong and Kimm and Ken Oostman for their support, love, and friendship. I am grateful for how you showed our family the love of Christ during a very difficult time in our lives. You will always have a special place in my heart.

I would like to thank my mom for showing me Jesus. Mom, your love for Him is a shining light for all to see and I want to thank you for all of your prayers that have made a huge difference in my life. I love you very much.

Thank you to Anita Pickelheimer for sharing the truth with me that our God is the God of the impossible, which set me on the course to freedom from bondage. I am forever grateful to you!

I would also like to sincerely thank Bonny San Hamel for prophesying a word to me that greatly encouraged me and gave me confidence to step out in the prophetic and set me on a path to hearing the Lord's voice more accurately at a crucial time in my life. The prophetic word from the Lord through Bonny has been a huge gift and I thank you for blessing me and many others in the Body of Christ.

I would like to say a special thanks to Patricia King for being such an encouragement to the Body of Christ in too many ways to list. Her joy of the Lord and love of the Father is contagious and shines through her wherever she goes and whenever she speaks. Thank you, Patricia, for your heart and dedication to be the hands and feet of Jesus not only to the Body of Christ, but also to lost and broken people around the world. You were created for such a time as this to be a blessing to many people.

I would also like to thank Carol Martinez of XP Publishing for her time, patience, and help during the process of publishing this book. In addition, I am very grateful for Jim Wies, my XP editor, for believing in this book. Jim, thank you very much for all of your encouragement, ideas, and wisdom that helped this book to come alive. You were a huge gift from the Lord during this whole process and a real joy to work with. I am very grateful for all you have done.

SPECIAL ACKNOWLEDGEMENTS

I would like to say a special thank you from my heart to Jeremy Lopez, founder of Identity Network, for his love, faithfulness, and dedication to the Body of Christ. Jeremy gave me a prophetic word in June 2009 that prophesied this devotional book. Part of the word is as follows:

The Lord said, "Daughter I want you to begin to start using your hands. For I have given you the power to write, and I have given you the power to begin to write things down." I hear the Lord say, "I'm even going to cause you to begin to write, you can call it poetry, you can call it love notes, you can call it whatever, but I have given you the power to write, daughter. I want you to start writing down things that I will place in your spirit."

"Daughter, you are going to begin to write things, and write things for other people," God said, "because other people need to know my love. Daughter, I want you to begin to write things down and send them out as letters to people who are hurting and going through a hard time." God said, "That way they can open up these letters in their own homes, in the privacy of their own home, and they will begin to read." And God said, "That way My Spirit can come in when it's just them and Me, and My Spirit will begin to draw them closer and let them understand how much I love them."

"Daughter, I have given you a writing ability and I want you to begin to execute. I want you to begin to carry out that command of writing not just for Me, daughter, but for My people as well."

And the Lord says, "Daughter, I've summoned you for such a time as this. You are not a mistake," says the Lord. "Yes, you have been in a place in your life where you have been rejected, and you know what it is like to be rejected. Even though I never ordained for you to walk through rejection, through that rejection and through that test, I will build a great testimony."

This word from our Heavenly Daddy through Jeremy strengthened and encouraged me numerous times during the course of writing this book. Jeremy, thank you for being such a blessing to the Body of Christ and using your incredible spiritual gifts to encourage and uplift Daddy's children. Thank you for prophesying our Heavenly Father's heart of love over the Body of Christ.

TABLE OF CONTENTS

Table of Contents

EDITOR'S FOREWORD

I was enthused when I was invited to write a foreword for this very inspiring volume by Nichole Marbach. There are many books available today ABOUT prophetic ministry but few that ARE prophetic ministry - prophetic ministry being simply defined as **"God talking to somebody, through somebody."** This book is one continuous prophetic feast and is literally page after page of edification, exhortation and comfort straight from the heart of God and His throne of grace.

But it is not for the hurried speed reader. Designed to be a daily devotional, each daily prophetic message needs to be pondered and savored and allowed to fully impact the reader with the messages of grace that are so adeptly communicated.

As you take the time to ponder these words, you will receive fresh insight as Nichole unveils the "Daddy" heart of God through these letters, and offers glimpse after glimpse into His heart of love and grace. And for those who want to grow in their own prophetic gifting, this book offers great examples of how God talks to His "kids" with words that are full of mercy and affection.

When one embraces the responsibility to be an oracle for God, it is of vital importance to first of all, know God's heart in order to rightly represent Him. Quite evident throughout this book is the fact that Nichole has drawn close to God and has captured His heart of unrelenting love, forgiveness and acceptance toward us, His children.

It is also true that the deepest messages are very often born out of the greatest struggles and most difficult trials of life. Nichole's own personal trials and triumph has given her some important things to say to the Body of Christ. Messages that are simple, yet simply profound. We should love God because He so deeply loves us. We should enjoy Him because He thoroughly enjoys us. We should offer unconditional love and acceptance to others because that is what He offers us. We should yearn for intimacy with Him because He so yearns for intimacy with us.

Thank you, Nichole, for caring enough for the Body of Christ to share out of your own personal moments of intimacy and insight the things that you have learned, visions you have received and the words you have heard from your Savior and Lord.

Jim Wies
XPPublishing/CSA

MY TESTIMONY OF HEALING

For years, I looked like a typical wife and mother who had it all together. I adored my children and was a stay at home mom. I also had a loving husband and we looked like we had a perfect life to everyone around us. However, after years of stuffing extreme emotional pain, I could no longer hold it in and pretend that everything was fine. I slowly started losing my mind. In addition to extreme anger and anxiety, including panic attacks and depression, I started numbing with alcohol on a daily basis so that I wouldn't feel the emotional pain or hear the racing voices in my head.

I was eventually diagnosed with alcoholism and many mental illnesses, including bipolar disorder by three different doctors. I was also addicted to self-injury and even received stitches in one of my wrists at one point. I was in so much pain that I didn't care if I lived or died. The voices in my head told me that I needed to punish myself for being such a horrible person who continually disappointed God and everyone around me. I even attempted to take my life and wrote too many goodbye letters to count. I felt so much guilt, shame, and self-hatred because all I wanted to do was self-destruct. The voices in my head told me my family would be better off without me, and I believed them. Even though I was a believer who had an incredible, supportive husband, three beautiful kids, many friends, and no financial worries, I felt no hope of ever being free from the constant torment in my mind.

 After many times in inpatient and outpatient therapy, I still struggled to find some peace and was suicidal almost every day for years. The temporary peace I felt after finishing different programs, meetings, medication changes, and therapy never lasted. I prayed and read the Bible whenever I could focus, yet I still could not find the peace I was desperately searching for. I also started bingeing on food almost every night to escape the mental torment and gained a lot of weight. All I wanted to do was escape the extreme emotional pain I could not get rid of, no matter how hard I tried.

I was told that the diseases I struggled with were incurable, so my only desire for years was for them to be managed enough to give me the desire to live for myself and my family. However, after years of many relapses and trying everything possible to find some lasting stability in my life, I finally received the revelation of this truth— that God didn't give me these sicknesses, and He wanted me well, and He alone is the way to true, lasting peace (Isaiah 53:5). I also learned that I was struggling with the kingdom of darkness (Ephesians 6:12), which wanted to steal, kill, and destroy me (John 10:10). I realized that only Jesus and His name, above all names, could set me free! I received the revelation that being a child of God entitled me to be able to kick the enemy out of my life because Jesus defeated him on the cross (Colossians 2:15). I finally understood that healing, not sickness, is part of the inheritance Jesus purchased for me on the cross. After kicking the enemy out of my life, I started learning how to take authority over him anytime he tries to come to steal something that is mine; especially my peace. I also had to learn to take every thought and lie of the enemy captive and renew my mind with the truth of the Word of God (2 Corinthians 10:4-5). The Word of God says that I have the "mind of Christ (1 Corinthians 2:16)" and a "sound mind (2 Timothy 1:7 - "For God hath not given us the spirit of fear; but of power, and of love, and of a sound mind." - KJ)." I chose to start putting my faith in the Word of God and started soaking up everything it says about my inheritance through Jesus Christ. I was amazed at all the things I didn't know were in the Bible about healing, deliverance, the kingdom of darkness, faith, etc., even though I had been going to church for most of my life. I continued and still continue to fill myself with the Lord's life-giving words of the Bible, which are life and healing to all who find them. (Proverbs 4:20-22).

After receiving healing and deliverance, I was finally ready and able to let Heavenly Father fill me with His passionate love. In addition, after suffering from insomnia almost my whole life to the extent that I required medication to sleep, I finally have the peace to be able to sleep through the night, medication free. I was also able to go off the numerous medications (up to 7 at one point) that I had to take every day for years and have been medication free for a number of years now. I believe with all of my heart that Jesus and His finished work of the cross is the way to true, lasting peace, healing, and wholeness.

Over the years that followed, I have hungered and cried out to the Lord in desperation for a deeper revelation of Christ's love, which is our inheritance in Christ. And my Heavenly Father has been more than faithful to answer. Experiencing His love and acceptance of me has shown me how to extend grace, love, and acceptance to myself instead of wanting to self-destruct. Being able to experience His love and knowing Him as My Daddy has been my greatest healing, setting me free to live an abundant life. My identity has also shifted from all of the labels I was given, to simply being a child of God. Receiving the truth of who I am in Christ more and more over the years has given me so much freedom to be the woman that He created me to be. I finally have the joy I was searching for deep down in my soul.

I have also learned that our Heavenly Daddy is not a God who sits on the throne constantly disappointed in His children with a frown on His face every time we fail. Rather, He is a God of joy who loves and accepts us all the time! He is in a great mood! He is so much fun to be around, and I can be myself with Him. He loves to play little jokes on me, and I have more fun with Him than anyone. Knowing His fun side has brought me so much happiness and healing. There is no one I would rather spend time with than Him, and this intimacy has totally set me free.

Our Heavenly Daddy has also shown me Jesus and the finished work of the cross, and what it means for me as a New Covenant child. Receiving revelation of what Jesus purchased for me has radically turned my mourning into dancing. Focusing on Jesus and His finished work of the cross (1 Corinthians 2:2) has filled me with a joy that I never knew existed. Keeping my eyes on Him rather than myself, has brought me peace, joy, and liberty and has helped me to experience His extreme love—the only way to true freedom and lasting peace. Knowing it will take me an eternity to grasp His amazing love, I continually hunger and pray for a deeper revelation of Jesus and His finished work. He is faithful to answer, and it continues to remain an exciting journey, filling my life with bliss and replacing the constant sorrow and depression I once felt. Life is good with Jesus!

No matter what situation you are in right now, never give up hope! Our God is the God of the impossible! He wants us to live a life that is beyond our wildest imaginations. He wants us to receive everything that Jesus purchased at Calvary and take back everything the enemy has stolen because of His passionate love for us. It is finished and done! Jesus did it all for us. What good news for God's beloved children!

~ Nichole Marbach

INTRODUCTION

Ephesians 3:16-19 (NLT) – "I pray that from his glorious, unlimited resources he will empower you with inner strength through his Spirit. Then Christ will make his home in your hearts as you trust in him. Your roots will grow down into God's love and keep you strong. And may you have the power to understand, as all God's people should, how wide, how long, how high, and how deep his love is. May you experience the love of Christ, though it is too great to understand fully. Then you will be made complete with all the fullness of life and power that comes from God."

This devotional book was created to be read daily and not all at once. I suggest that you read one daily devotional and then do the journaling for that day. The various journaling exercises will help draw you into deeper intimacy with Heavenly Daddy, Jesus, and Holy Spirit. I recommend that you take as much time as you need each day soaking up these words and visions, doing the exercises, and meditating on the Scriptures. My prayer is that you will be blessed, touched, and forever transformed by receiving a deeper revelation of the Father's love. If that is your desire, say the following prayer:

Heavenly Daddy, I pray that Your Holy Spirit will touch me as I am reading these precious words from You. I pray that emotional healing would take place and that these words would sink deep into my spirit. May I receive a deeper revelation of the burning, passionate love of Christ for me. May I know You as "Daddy" and be transformed from the inside out. Father, let these words break off any lies that I have been believing about You. I pray that I would experience Your peace, joy, and love until it overflows in my life. May I see myself through Your eyes. In Jesus' precious name, Amen!

~Day 1~

I WILL NOT LEAVE YOU AS ORPHANS

"Come to Me, My children, My precious children. Let the fatherless and the abandoned ones come to Me, and I will comfort them. I am the God of all comfort. Come, let Me love you the way you were destined to be loved. Come, let Me heal your broken, wounded hearts. Come, let Me hold you in My loving arms the way you were meant to be held.

"Let Me lavish My love on you. Let Me fill the void left by the wounds of your earthly fathers. I am your Father, but I love it when you call Me 'Daddy.' In the name 'Daddy' is intimacy and relationship. Don't be afraid to call Me your Daddy, your Abba Father.

"There is healing for you when you cry out 'Daddy.' There is security for you when you cry out, 'Daddy.' There is joy for you when you realize that I am your Daddy. There is victory for you when you cry out, 'Daddy!'

"I created you to be My child so that I could love on you, take care of you, and be in intimate relationship with you. Come, rest in your Heavenly Daddy's arms right now."

Psalm 68:5; Isaiah 9:6; Galatians 4:6; John 14:18; Psalm 34:18; Psalm 103:13

Prayer:

Heavenly Father, I want to know You as my Heavenly Daddy. I want the intimacy that is in the word "Daddy." Daddy, I pray that You would heal all of my childhood wounds with Your love and that You would fill the void that no earthly father could ever fill. Help me to know You as the only perfect parent that can provide for all of my needs. From this moment on, I will think of You as my "Daddy." In Jesus' name, Amen.

*Keep saying throughout the day, "I have the best Daddy in the world. I am His precious, beloved child that He adores. My identity is in being His child. I am His favored one."

Spend some time writing your Heavenly Father a letter
telling Him that you want to know Him as "Daddy."

~Day 2~

LET ME BE YOUR DADDY!

"Child, I want to be the Daddy you have always dreamed of having. I want to show you that I have always thought of you as My special child that I dearly desired. Your name is even engraved on the palm of My hand, and I show it off in Heaven! No one can remove your name from My hand, no one! Do you know that I even talk about you? I talk about how special you are to Me. You are always on My mind. You never leave My thoughts. You never leave My eyes. That is how special you are to Me.

"Come to Me! Let Me be your Daddy. Come talk to Me. Come cry to Me. Come and let Me hold you until you realize I am holding you like a father holds a child in his arms of protection.

"Come under My wings! I will protect you from the storms of life. Under My wings, you will find rest during the storms. Only under My wings will you find the rest and peace you have been searching for. I protect you even more than an eagle protects her babies in the nest. That protective instinct that humans and animals feel towards their babies comes from Me. That is how I feel about you, but My love and protection is so much greater. You are a special treasure that I want to protect. Come under My wings, and you will feel Me protecting you and keeping you safe."

Isaiah 49:16; John 10:29; Psalm 91

Prayer:

Heavenly Daddy, thank You for reminding me that I am not a mistake and I was truly Your desire. Thank You for reminding me that I am special in Your eyes and I never leave Your thoughts. Help me to remember that, under Your wings, I will find rest and peace through all the storms that come my way. Father, help me to feel Your loving arms of love around me right now. In Jesus' precious name, Amen.

*Spend some time thanking Him for being your Daddy. If you are still feeling wounded in any way about your earthly father, give it over to Him today and let Him fill that void and heal you. Let Him show you that He is the best Daddy you could ever have. Tell Him how much you need Him and feel His heartbeat of love for you.

Journal about what it means to you to be under the wings of your Heavenly Daddy. Do you feel His love and protection? Talk to Him about it.

~Day 3~

CHILD, COME AND STAY AWHILE!

"My precious child whom I adore, come and sit with Me and stay awhile. I long for your presence. Child, when you sit at My feet, stay! Stay for awhile! Often, you are rushed, and you become distracted with all you need to do for the day. However, I say come and sit awhile and let Me bless you and fill you with My presence and strength so that you can effortlessly make it through the day.

"Come and let Me give you your daily manna. I am the bread of life! In your daily manna, I have provided everything you need. Come, receive your daily spiritual food. Each day I will give you something new and different. Come, take and receive your spiritual nourishment for the day. Come in My presence and receive what you need. The only thing I ask is that you stay awhile.

"Beloved, sometimes distractions take you away from receiving all that I want to give you for the day. Sometimes I prompt you to stay so that I can give you wisdom for the moment and share what I have planned for you, but you say, 'I must go. I have a busy day today.' Beloved, this does not make Me love you any less. However, when you are rushed to leave, you miss out on the blessings of true intimacy and fellowship with Me.

"I am your Heavenly Daddy and I long to give you many revelations, secrets, and truths when you sit with Me. Come, stay awhile, and you will be abundantly blessed. Come, stay awhile, and you will be abundantly filled with all you need for each day. I long for your presence. Come and stay awhile!"

Exodus 16; John 6:35

Prayer:

Heavenly Daddy, today I choose to sit with You awhile so that I can be blessed and filled with all that You want me to receive. While I am sitting with You, I will let go of all distractions and "to do" lists so that I can focus my attention on You alone. Father, I pray that You would give me a hunger for more of Your presence that can only be satisfied when I am with You. Thank You for my daily manna. In Jesus' name, Amen.

*Spend some intimate time alone with your Heavenly Daddy today. Ask Him to share a secret with you. Sit in His presence. Picture yourself seated in Heavenly places with Him because that is where you are seated right now.

Write down anything Daddy shares with you today
and tell Him what is on your heart.

~Day 4~

THE LOVE GIFT FROM EAST TO WEST

I saw a vision of Jesus. He had an enormous present that was so high and so wide that I could not see where it ended. The present went as far as the East is from the West. He told me that this present represented His unending love He has for His people. Next, I saw myself give Him a present. It was very tiny, the size of a ring box. He told Me that it represented the love I have for Him. I was disappointed when I heard that. However, when He opened up my small gift, He was ecstatic. He was jumping up and down with joy. I have never seen Him so excited. Next, I heard these words:

"My beloved, I know your heart's desire is to love Me with all of your heart, mind, and soul. I also know that the enemy enjoys telling you that your love for Me is nothing. He tells you that you have failed in that area and that I am displeased with your love. Beloved, those are lies. I know your heart, and I am so pleased with the love you are capable of giving Me. It brings Me so much joy when My precious children give Me their love and devotion.

"My beloved, when you understand My love for you, your love for Me, yourself, and others will increase. You won't have to force yourself to do it, it will just happen. I want you to learn to rest in My love for you. Let Me take down all the walls of hurt you have experienced in your life. Let Me show you that it is safe to love Me. I won't let you down. Let Me saturate you with My love right now. Go into the secret place and wait. Wait on Me and let Me bless you with My unending love gift. It brings Me joy to pour out My love on you."

Matthew 22:37-40

Prayer:

Heavenly Daddy, my heart's desire is to love You with all of my heart, my mind, and my soul. I realize that I cannot do this until I take down all of the walls that are preventing me from truly receiving Your love. Daddy, help me to see what walls I have up and help me to remove them so I can receive my inheritance. In Jesus' name, Amen.

*Spend some time today telling your Father how much you love Him and thank Him for His unconditional love for you.

Write a letter to Daddy telling Him how much you want to know and experience His love for you.

~Day 5~

DO YOU HEAR ME?

I want to give some background for this devotional. I live in the Chicago area. In 2007, the cicadas started emerging from the ground during a period of three weeks. They only emerge once every 17 years. This was all over the news. Everyone was talking about it. Once they emerged, that is all you could hear everywhere you went. They are very noisy insects. During this time, the Lord gave me a dream. He sounded very grieved in the dream, and it touched my heart. He said, "When people hear the cicadas, they know it is the cicadas' voices speaking, but many of these people don't even know the voice of their Creator. They don't know My voice. They don't know what I sound like. Many of My children know the voice of insects more than Mine." My heart was aching as I woke up. I felt His longing for His children to really know His voice. Then I heard these words:

"My sweet treasure, do you hear Me when I call your name? I want you to know My voice in the same way you know the voices of your friends and loved ones. We were destined to have an intimate relationship together. I long for you to know My voice. Precious one, in the same way you hear the birds singing or the crickets chirping and you know it is their voices, I want you to recognize the sound of My voice.

"When you know My voice, you hear Me giving you wisdom and guidance for your every need and situation. When you hear Me telling you how much I love you and what My Son did for you, you will get a revelation that I am truly for you, not against you, and you will live a life of victory.

"Beloved, relationships involve two-way communication. Sometimes, I enjoy it when you stop talking to Me and just listen for My still small voice responding to what you have told Me. I will show you more and more what I sound like when you enter the secret place. I have been speaking to you since you were in your mother's womb, and I will continue to talk to you for all eternity. Do you hear Me calling you now? Come, let's spend some time conversing together."

John 10:27

Prayer:

Heavenly Daddy, help me to discern Your voice speaking to Me. Help me to know Your voice in the same way I know the voices of my loved ones. Prompt me to stop talking and just listen sometimes so that I can hear what You want to share with Me. In Jesus' name, Amen.

Write a letter to Daddy telling Him that you want to know
His voice more than any other.

_____

_____

_____

_____

_____

_____

_____

_____

_____

_____

_____

_____

_____

_____

_____

_____

_____

_____

_____

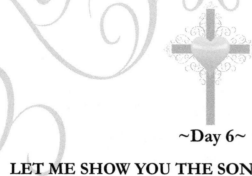

~Day 6~

LET ME SHOW YOU THE SONG I SING OVER YOU

"Child, come and listen! Listen carefully to Me. I want to share a song with you. I want you to listen carefully to the words. It is a song that I continually sing over you. Do your hear it? Come closer and let Me share it with you. It is a unique song created just for you. Come and listen! I am softly singing a love song over you telling you how much you mean to Me. Get a pen! Write it down! This is a song created specifically for you. I want to bless you and show you what I have been singing over you.

"Come, listen! I will show you the song. Come, listen to its life-giving words of love over you. This is a love song for My lover. I want you to receive the words deep into your spirit so that My love can transform you and heal you.

"Come, receive the song I sing over you. Listen carefully. It is a faint love song that you alone will hear because it is uniquely created for you. Come, receive your love song straight from My heart to yours. The words are a weapon against discouragement and depression. The words are a weapon against the kingdom of darkness. The lyrics will extinguish the fiery darts of the enemy in your life. These love lyrics I created for you will cause the enemy to flee. He cannot stand to hear these words of love and truth I give to you.

"Beloved, can you hear Me singing now? Come closer and listen. I am singing over you right now."

John 14:26; Zephaniah 3:17

Prayer:

Precious Father, I pray that You will share with me the lyrics to the song that You are continually singing over me. I come by faith with a pen ready to write down these life-giving words. I will use them as a weapon against the enemy in my life. I will read these words to remind myself and renew my mind with how much You love me and how You truly see me. I am coming closer to listen and to learn this new love song You have for me. I can't wait to hear it! In Jesus' name, Amen.

*After you have heard the song from Daddy to you, on the next page, write a love song to Him and then sing it to Him. Feel His tender heart of love towards you. Feel how pleased He is with your worship.

Write a love song from your heart to your Heavenly Daddy.

~Day 7~

I LOVE TO LAUGH WITH YOU!

"Oh, how I wish My children knew how much fun I would like to have with them! I love to laugh and have fun, and, yes, I even have a sense of humor. I even love to play little jokes on My children and have a good time with them. I love to make My children laugh. When they realize it is Me making them laugh and having fun with them, I increase those times of joy that we have together.

"My children, come! Come discover that I am enjoyable to be around. Come discover that you can be yourself in My presence. Come and make Me laugh. Let's laugh together and have fun.

"Come, let's even laugh at the enemy. He is the opposite of joy. When you are in the midst of a trial, he hates it when he sees us laughing together. He hates to see you full of joy in My presence. He hates the sound of joy and laughter so much that he flees from it.

"Come, child, let's laugh together and have fun!"

Psalm 2:4; Psalm 16:11

Prayer:

Heavenly Daddy, I don't know Your sense of humor the way that I want to. Help me to see You as My loving Father that loves to have fun with me and make me laugh. Help me to know when You are the one playing little jokes on me to help me to see Your sense of humor. God, I want to know You in this way. I also want to make You laugh. I want to have fun with You. I want to discover in a deeper way Your fun side. Help me to just relax and be myself in Your presence. Thank You, Daddy, for loving me so much that You want to make me laugh and experience Your joy. You are my joy! In Jesus' name, Amen.

*Ask your Heavenly Daddy to show you something funny today that you know is from Him. Laugh and have fun together. Joy comes from Him.

Write a letter to your Daddy telling Him how much you want to know His fun side and sense of humor.

~Day 8~

DON'T BE AFRAID TO ASK ME FOR ANYTHING

"My precious child, I want you to start asking Me for the desires of your heart, all of them. Don't hold any of them back from Me. I already know the desires of your heart. I know which ones you ask Me for, and I know which ones you hold back from asking. Child, I love to give you good gifts, and I love to answer your prayers.

"Beloved, sometimes you hesitate. You were not used to getting your needs and desires met by your earthly parents. You were afraid to ask for things and that has carried over into our relationship. Precious one, I am not like earthly parents. Many of My children who are parents were wounded when they were children and that carried over into their parenting. The result is generational wounds that keep passing down from generation to generation. I want to heal every single wound that has ever been passed down. Child, that wound and fear you felt when asking your parents for your desires, let Me heal it. Come to Me! Let My love take away your fear to ask Me for the desires of your heart. I long for My children to trust Me and understand that I am good. I love to give them the desires of their hearts when they come and ask Me.

"Beloved, sometimes you have not because you ask not. Come to Me and tell Me your dreams, passions, and desires. Do you know that some of those desires you fear asking Me about even come from Me? Come and find out in the secret place. Come and see that some things you are asking for have already been accomplished for you by My Son on the cross. I am not withholding! Come into the secret place and let Me show you what is already yours. Let Me take all doubt and unbelief from you. Just ask Me! I love it when you ask Me for your desires. I love to give you abundantly more than you could ever imagine because you are My precious child, and I am your good Heavenly Daddy!"

Luke 11:11; 1 John 4:18; Psalm 37:4; James 4:2; Ephesians 3:20

Prayer:

Heavenly Daddy, I am going to start asking You for all of the desires of my heart. I will not hold back due to fear or fear of rejection from You, which is the ploy of the enemy. I ask that You heal all of my childhood wounds and continue to show me that You are the perfect parent I have desired my whole life. Thank You for caring about my desires. You are so precious to me. In Jesus' name, Amen.

Spend some time writing your Heavenly Daddy a letter asking Him
for the desires of your heart and what you need from Him.
Don't hold back. He knows everything you need even before you speak.

~Day 9~

I LONG TO BE YOUR BEST FRIEND

"Child, no other can love you like I do. No other has your best interests at heart like I do. No other friendship can satisfy you the way My friendship can satisfy you. I will never reject you! I will never disappoint you! I will never let you down! I will never wound you! My love is unconditional, and you do not need to work for it!

"Precious one, I long to be your best friend. I want you to share your deepest secrets with Me, and I want to share My deepest secrets with you. I want you to share your burdens with Me and let Me carry them for you. I want to give you wisdom and insight to help you with your problems and struggles. I want to be the best friend you have been longing for.

"Dear friend, come to Me. I can make you smile and laugh. Come, let's spend time together. Let's go for a walk together and converse the whole time. Let Me show you what I see. Let Me show you the world through My eyes.

"I long for intimacy with you. I long for deep, deep fellowship with you. I long to be your best friend. You were created for intimacy with Me. You were made to be loved by Me.

"My favored one, I was willing to empty Myself and give My life up for you to give you an abundant life filled with everything you need. Precious one, I live in you. You will never find a more loyal friend than Me. I live in you. Not only do I live in you, but because I live in you, everything you will ever need lives in you, too.

"Come, your best friend is waiting. I'm waiting to share My world with you. I have so much to tell you. I am overjoyed for you to come into My presence so that I can bless you and fill you to the overflow."

Exodus 33:11; Psalm 34:8

Prayer:

Jesus, I want to know You as my best friend. I want to be able to come to You with everything in my life, the good and the bad, and know that You love me unconditionally and will never reject me. Show me how to have fun with You and how to be myself in Your holy presence. Teach me how to be vulnerable with You. I desire to know You as my best friend. Show me the world through Your eyes. In Your name, Amen.

Spend some time telling Jesus about any friendship hurts you have had and let Him heal the wounds. Write Him a letter from your heart telling Him why you want Him to be your best friend and touch His heart.

_____

_____

_____

_____

_____

_____

_____

_____

_____

_____

_____

_____

_____

_____

_____

_____

_____

_____

_____

~Day 10~

I FOCUS ON WHAT'S RIGHT WITH YOU

"My beloved, do not listen to the voices that want you to dwell on the negative. Ignore the voices that want to keep you focused on all your present and past trials and sorrows. Self-pity wants to keep you focused on yourself and everything that is wrong with you. The enemy knows that when he gets you into self-pity, he has you in a trap of depression and despair.

"My precious child, I want you to focus on Jesus and what He did for you. When you keep your eyes on Him, you can't help but get rid of self-pity. When you focus on Jesus, you are focusing on what is right and all that is right with you. My Son took your sin and gave you His righteousness. Child, you are right with Me. I see you as righteous as My Son. When you focus on these truths from My Word, you will see self-pity disappear from your life.

"Beloved, I want you to renew your mind with what is right with you, not what is wrong with you. Because of the finished work of Jesus, I focus on what is right with you. The enemy continues to focus on what is wrong with you. When the enemy wins, you are filled with hopelessness and discouragement. When I win, you are filled with joy, peace, and love. Child, what will you choose? Let Me help you choose what is right.

"You are so precious to Me. That is what I focus on. I love you, precious child. You are so beautiful to Me. Renew your mind with this TRUTH."

Hebrews 12:2; 2 Corinthians 5:21; Romans 12:2; Colossians 2:22-23

Prayer:

Heavenly Daddy, help me to see where self-pity may be manifesting in my life. I want to get rid of it. It brings me into a cycle of depression to focus on negative things and everything that is wrong with me. Help me to renew my mind with the truth of how You see me and my true identity in Christ. I ask You to heal any wounds that may have been an open door for self-pity to come in. Nothing is too big for You. You are the God of the impossible. I choose to close the door on self-pity and get rid of it in Jesus' name, Amen.

*Spend some time meditating on all of the things that are right with you because of what Jesus did.

Write down all of the positive qualities about your personality and then write a letter to Daddy telling Him how much you want to be able to love yourself and extend yourself some grace.

~Day 11~

I THOUGHT OF YOU THAT DAY!

"Beloved, I thought of you at Calvary. Precious one, you never left my mind as I willingly gave My body to be punished for you. With every single lash, I thought, 'This is so My precious children can experience joy and peace.' With every lash, I thought, 'This is so My precious children can be healed and live the abundant life.' With every lash, I thought, 'This is so My children will truly see how much I love them.'

"Precious one, if you ever doubt My love for you, I want you to picture what I went through because of My unending, everlasting, extreme love for you. The emotional pain I endured, even sweating drops of blood, does not compare to the love I have for you. The torture I went through as I experienced every evil sin and demonic power was nothing compared to the great love I have for you.

"Beloved, it brings Me great joy when My children realize how much I love and adore them. I love it when My children receive forgiveness and healing because of what I went through at Calvary. Even the angels rejoice whenever My children get a glimpse of the great love I have for them.

"Child, receive these words in your heart. I love you. I love you. I love you. I love you. I could not love you any more than I do right now. You will always be My beloved, no matter what you do or don't do. Let this truth sink in and set you free. I love you!"

Isaiah 53:5; John 10:10; 15:13; Luke 22:43-44

Prayer:

Heavenly Daddy, Thank You for Your great love for me. Whenever the enemy attacks me with doubt that You love me, remind me of the cross and what Jesus willingly did for me all because of His extreme love. Thank You, precious Jesus, for what You went through for me. In Your name, Amen.

 *Spend some time lifting up the precious name of Jesus right now and be filled with His precious love. Picture Him smiling at you because that is what He is doing right now. Picture Him gazing into your beautiful eyes as you worship Him. Picture His heart melting as He listens to your worship. Feel His love. Feel His arms wrapped around you.

Write a letter to Jesus thanking Him for the suffering
He endured for you on the cross.

~Day 12~

I DO NOT CONDEMN YOU WHEN YOU SIN!

"My precious child, I do not condemn you when you sin. The enemy tells you that you are not worthy to be in My presence when you sin. That is a lie. I tell you to come boldly into My presence in your time of need. Come to My throne of grace and come boldly, not full of shame and condemnation. Child, Jesus took all of your sin and punishment on the cross. He did it out of His great love for you. Nothing you ever do catches Me by surprise. I know everything you will ever do. I see all of your victories, and I see all of your failures, yet I do not love you any less when you fail. In fact, I want to pour out my love on you even more when you fail so that my love and grace will transform your failures into victories.

"Beloved, you MUST get the revelation that I do not condemn you when you fail. When you understand what Jesus did for you, you will stop striving to stop sinning. Child, when you strive to continue to live under the law, it only causes disappointment and failure. Then you believe the lie that I am disappointed in you because you failed. Precious one, when you understand that you are living under a New Covenant of grace and not under the law, you will experience peace and rest, and your striving will cease. You will effortlessly have more victories, and you will effortlessly say no to temptations to sin. When you get the revelation that I love you no matter what, I do not condemn you when you fail, and Jesus took your wrath on the cross, it will help you to lead a holy life. There is no condemnation for those who belong in My Kingdom.

"I do not condemn you! Rather, I tell you that I see you as holy and blameless because of the shed blood of Jesus. Let this truth set you free from all guilt and condemnation in your life."

Romans 8:1; Hebrews 4:16; 2 Corinthians 5:21; Romans 6:14; Colossians 1:22; Ephesians 1:4

Prayer:

Father, I desire the revelation that you do not condemn me when I fail, rather, You want to pour Your love out on me even more. Help me to go boldly into Your presence in my time of need to receive all that I need. Help me to let go of all self-condemnation in my life. Open my heart to receive the love and acceptance You have for me so that I can live a holy life. In Jesus' name, Amen.

*Spend some time thanking Jesus from your heart that He became your sin on the cross and took it away for you. Write at least five times, "Jesus took all of my sin, and, in exchange, He gave me His righteousness at the cross. Therefore, My Heavenly Daddy never condemns me when I sin." Let it really sink in.

Write a letter to Daddy thanking Him for sending
Jesus to take your cup of wrath.

~Day 13~

I WILL ALWAYS BE FAITHFUL TO YOU, MY BRIDE!

I saw a vision of a woman crying. She was heartbroken because her husband committed adultery. I saw Jesus. He came and took her in His arms. He put a ring on her finger. He held her hand. He took her head in His hands, and, as He was gazing into her tear-stained eyes, I heard Him say these words:

"My beloved, I will never, ever be unfaithful to you. You belong to Me. You are My bride. I will never leave you for another. I will never break your heart. I will never let you go. You can trust Me, My bride. You can trust Me. I am the only one that will never let you down. I will never divorce you. I will never leave you. I will never break My covenant with you! People may wound you and hurt you and cause you much pain, but I will never do that to you. In fact, let Me take your pain and suffering. Let Me put it at the foot of the cross. I carried your sorrows that day. I carried them for you. I love you so much, and I want you to give all of your pain to Me. Give Me the heartache. Give Me the wounds. Give it all to Me. Give Me your heart. Precious one, give Me your heart. Let Me heal your wounded heart. Give Me your heart, and you will not regret it. You were created to be My bride. You were created to have intimacy and relationship with Me. Trust Me, beloved, with your whole heart. Surrender your whole heart to Me. Let Me show you My faithfulness. Let Me show you how committed I am to our relationship. I will never break my covenant with you, never! Let Me show you that I am the one Who will take care of you more than any other. Let Me take that wounded, broken heart and heal it so it can love again. Let My fiery love ignite your heart to love again. Let My love heal you. Beloved, you were created to be loved by Me, and you were created to love others.

"Precious one, I am the God of the impossible. I love to take messes and make them into miracles. If you are believing for supernatural breakthrough in your marriage, don't give up hope. I can restore and heal any situation. Keep believing for your miracle and watch what I can do. Keep trusting that I have plans to prosper you and not to harm you. I will always remain faithful to you, My beloved bride."

Isaiah 53:4; 1 Corinthians 1:9; Psalm 36:5; Hebrews 13:5; 2 Chronicles 16:9; 1 John 4:19; Genesis 17:7; Jeremiah 29:11; Isaiah 54:5

Prayer:

Jesus, You are the only one that can heal the pain I have experienced from people rejecting me. I give it to You now. Thank You that You will never, ever leave me nor forsake me. Thank You for Your eternal faithfulness. In Your name, Amen.

Write a letter to Jesus telling Him how much you want to know Him as your faithful husband that will never leave you or hurt you.

*If a spouse has ever been unfaithful to you, spend some time asking Daddy to heal any wounds that came in during that time. If you need to, pray for supernatural breakthrough in your marriage. Picture Jesus as your faithful husband who will never ever leave you. Let this truth fill you with His peace and love. Picture yourself giving Him your whole heart.

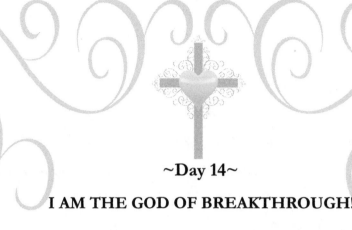

~Day 14~

I AM THE GOD OF BREAKTHROUGH!

"My child, I have seen your struggles. I have seen your tears. I have seen your pain. I have seen your frustration. I have heard you say, 'Is this all there is in this life, this fallen world?' I have counted your tears, and I keep track of them in Heaven. Not one tear is overlooked by Me. I hear all of your cries, every single one of them. You have never left My embrace. My arms are constantly wrapped around you, and My embrace grows even tighter during your times of pain and sorrow.

"I tell you breakthrough is about to happen. I am the God of breakthrough. Never give up hope, for hopelessness is the tactic of the evil one to lie to My children. The evil one wants you to think that I am not good to you. He wants you to think that I enjoy seeing you suffer. Child, My heart aches when I see My children in pain. My heart aches when My children give up hope. My heart aches when My children are deceived into thinking, 'breakthrough must not be for me, I don't deserve it.'

"Beloved, your breakthrough was purchased at the cross with the blood of Jesus. Your breakthrough is based on the blood alone. I am no respecter of persons. I love ALL of My children with an everlasting love and breakthrough is for every single one of them.

"You are eternally forgiven. Child, don't let the enemy defeat you with any guilt, condemnation, or your past. I love you so much that I sent Him to give you life and to take away all of your shame and guilt forever.

"Precious one, put your hope in Me. I love you so much. You are welcome to come boldly to My throne of grace and simply say, 'Daddy, I need a breakthrough.' Come and ask your Heavenly Daddy for what you need. I am waiting with open arms."

Psalm 56:8; Psalm 103:12; Hebrews 8:12; Hebrews 4:16

Prayer:

Heavenly Daddy, thank You for reminding me that breakthrough belongs to me, and You are not withholding it from me. Jesus, thank You for purchasing my breakthrough with Your blood. In Your name, Amen.

*If you need a breakthrough in any area of your life, picture yourself going boldly to the throne of grace and saying, "Daddy I need a breakthrough in _____ area of my life and start decreeing breakthrough in that area today.

Write down all the areas in which you desire breakthrough in your life.

Then, start writing down faith-filled decrees

in these areas and let your faith arise.

~Day 15~

I WILL PROVIDE A WAY OUT!

"My precious child, I know all about that sin, that sin that has become a bad habit that you do but don't want to do. I know how much guilt and shame you feel about it because the enemy comes and pounds you with it. I see how you are afraid to face Me each time you fail. My precious child, it is in these moments that I want you to run into My loving arms. Let Me show you how much I love you. Let Me show you that I look at your heart. I see your desire to stop sinning. Let Me help you, My beloved.

"Child, the shame you feel about that overwhelming desire to sin keeps you away from Me, your solution. I tell you that there is no temptation too big for Me to rescue you from. I WILL provide a way out for you each and every time if you come to Me and desire for Me to help you.

"I want you to get a deep revelation that your sinful nature died on the cross with Jesus. It was actually circumcised at the cross! 'In Him also you were circumcised with a circumcision not made with hands, but in a [spiritual] circumcision [performed by] Christ by stripping off the body of flesh (the whole corrupt, carnal nature with its passion and lusts)' (Colossians 2:11 AMP). Your old man died. You are a new creation. When you are tempted, say to yourself, 'I am dead to this sin. Christ lives in me, and I now live by the Spirit.'

"Come to Me when you feel temptation. I WILL provide a way out! Even if you fail, I want you to come to Me and let Me love on you. Precious beloved, I want to heal the root of why you do this sin when you don't want to. Let Me heal any pain that came in when you were a child. Come to Me, and I will help you, heal you, and show you the way to victory."

1 Corinthians 10:13; 2 Corinthians 5:17; Romans 6:6; 7:4-6; Colossians 2:11-12

Prayer:

Heavenly Daddy, help me to see that You are truly the answer to all of my problems. Help me to come to You when I am tempted to sin. Help me to battle all shame and guilt from the enemy that wants to keep me away from You during the time that I need You most. Thank You for helping me to overcome all temptation. Thank You, Jesus, for taking my sinful nature away on the cross and making me a new creation. Daddy, help me to rely on Christ in me to get through everything. Amen.

*Spend some time lifting up the name of Jesus until you feel His joy. Any time sin is knocking at your door, go to Him, and He will provide a way out for you.

Write down any sin issues you struggle with. Next to them, write, "Jesus took _____ as far as the East is from the West on the cross for me." Write Daddy a letter thanking Him for providing a way out each time temptation comes in. Tell Him how you want His Spirit in you to overcome temptation each time it arises. Thank Him for the victory!

~Day 16~

YOU ARE THE ONE I WANT!

"Yes, beloved, YOU are the one I love. YOU are the one I would do anything for, including giving up My life. I emptied Myself to come down and give My life for YOU.

"You are so precious to Me. I know exactly what you are thinking right now. I know every detail about your life. YOU are the one I love.

"YOU are the one I want to fellowship with right now. YOUR voice is the one I want to hear. Your voice is like a sweet fragrance going up to Heaven, and your words melt My heart. YOU are the one I want to be with right now.

"YOU are the one I want to share My heart with. YOU are the one I want to share My secrets with. You are the one I want to hold. YOU are the one I want to sing to. YOU are the one I want to whisper 'I love you' to. You are the one!

"Child, receive these life giving words and truth in your heart. Come into the secret place and let Me pour out My love on you and show you that YOU are the one I want and no one can ever take you away from Me."

1 John 3:1; Jeremiah 33:3; Proverbs 4:20-22

Prayer:

Dear Heavenly Daddy, thank You so much for reminding me that I'm the one You want. I am the one You sent Jesus to die for. I am the one You want to have an intimate relationship with. Thank You for continuing to pour out Your love on me. Thank You for renewing my mind with the truth that You love me so much and I am Your precious child. In Jesus' name, Amen.

*Read this devotional slowly several times. Really meditate on the words from your Heavenly Daddy to you and let them sink into your Spirit.

Spend some time writing your Heavenly Father a letter telling Him why He is the one you want. He will be touched by your precious words.

~Day 17~

YOU WERE NOT CREATED TO SUFFER ABUSE!

"My precious, precious child, I saw what happened to you. I want you to know that it broke My heart to see what the enemy did to you through a human vessel. Beloved, I saw the abuse you endured, and it grieved Me beyond words. I saw the torment, hurt, and pain you endured at the hands of people you trusted. Child, this was the enemy's plan to steal and destroy your life. This was never My plan for you. I do not cause My children to be abused. I am so grieved by what happened to you and My heart aches for what you endured.

"Precious one, let Me wipe away your tears. Let Me heal all of the wounds you endured when you were abused. Child, the fear, the anxiety, and the lack of trust you feel come from the enemy. I tell you that I am the way to complete freedom! The enemy wants to keep you in bondage, but I want to set you free! Let Me take the fear and all the other chains that came in and replace them with peace, joy, and love for Me and others. Let Me remove all the lies from the pit that say, 'I am unworthy, I am abnormal, I don't deserve love from anyone,' and replace them with the truth. The truth is that you are worthy. You are beautiful. You are righteous. You are completely cleansed because of what Jesus did for you. You are so worthy to receive My love and the love of others around you. Let Me turn your pain into a powerful testimony. I can turn all the evil acts of the enemy into something good and powerful. Come, let Me heal your wounds. I am the only way to healing and freedom. You are in My arms right now, and I will hold you as we both weep together. Then, I will wipe away your tears and turn your mourning into dancing! I will transform you with My love."

John 10:10; Isaiah 61:1; Romans 5:9; 5:17; 8:28

Prayer:

Heavenly Daddy, it is still painful to think about what I suffered at the hands of the enemy. Help me to see that it was the enemy. Help me to completely forgive the people that were used by the kingdom of darkness in my life. I choose to release them so that I can be set free. Daddy, come and heal the wounds. Come, show Me that I can trust You. I believe that You are the only one that can set me free from the bondage of abuse. I choose to let You heal me of every single wound. In Jesus' precious name, Amen.

*Spend some time crying out to the Lord about any past abuse if you are still feeling any wounds related to it. Let Him heal you today.

If you have suffered any type of abuse in your life, spend some time writing a letter to your Daddy telling Him how you felt. If you felt abandoned by Him, write it down and get it out. Then, break that lie and thank Him that this was not His plan for you and tell Him that you know He has plans to prosper you and not harm you. Write down all the hurts that you want to give to Him right now. Thank Jesus for taking all of these hurts for you on the cross and for never leaving you or forsaking you. Ask Him to shower His love on you in a special way today.

_____

_____

_____

_____

_____

_____

_____

_____

_____

_____

_____

_____

_____

_____

~Day 18~

I THIRSTED THAT DAY SO THAT YOU NEVER WOULD AGAIN

I saw a vision of Jesus. He was carrying the cross. He was in agony. The cross was causing Him so much pain as it was heavy bearing down on His open wounds. He was in pain. I saw His mouth. He was taking deep breaths, trying to swallow, but He couldn't swallow anything. His tongue was stuck to the roof of His mouth from the lack of having anything to drink. I saw sweat all over Him. The hot sun was beating down on Him, and He was very, very thirsty. I knew He was saying that He wanted something to drink. His mouth was so dry, and He was exhausted. Then I heard these words:

"My beloved, I thirsted that day so that you would never, ever thirst again. It was very painful not to be able to drink anything, but I did it for you. I am your river of living water. Come to Me whenever you are thirsty, whenever you feel dried out. Come to Me, and I will refresh you with My presence. Stay in My presence and come to Me, and you will never thirst again! I am the one who refreshes. I am the one who brings you life. Come to Me and let Me refresh you. Let Me bring life back into you. Are you thirsty?

"Come into My presence and let Me fill you with encouragement. Let Me fill you with revelation. Let Me fill you with breakthrough. Let Me fill you with healing. Let Me fill you with My glory. Let Me fill you with peace. What do you need? Bring your cup and let Me fill it with whatever you need. Tell Me what you need, child. Tell Me what you need right now and bring your cup and let Me fill it.

"Child, hold out your cup. Do you see what I am doing? Picture yourself holding it up above your head. Do you see the blood pouring into the cup overflowing unto your whole body. Do you feel My blood? You are covered with My blood. There is healing in the blood. There is forgiveness in the blood. There is victory in the blood. There is everything you need. I shed My blood for you. Child, don't ever forget that even if you were the only one on the earth, I would have endured everything just for you. I shed My precious, healing blood just for you. Because of My shed blood, you can come boldly to the throne of grace and ask for what you need!"

Psalm 22:15; John 7:37-39; John 19:28; Hebrews 10:19; Isaiah 55:1

Prayer:

Thank You Jesus for what You endured for me. Thank You for shedding Your blood so that I would lack nothing. As I come into Your presence, I ask that You would fill me with everything I need for the day. In Your name, Amen.

Picture Jesus saying, "Anyone who is thirsty, come to Me and drink..."
Write a letter to Jesus telling Him how thirsty you are for more of Him.
Tell Him how much you need a drink. Share your heart.
Thank Him for being the only one who can satisfy your thirst.

~Day 19~

MY LOVE BUBBLES UP AND OUT OVER THE UNIVERSE!

"My beloved, I want you to know that I am so filled with love. I am love. That is who I am. I am so filled with love that I can't help but pour it out onto My creation. It just bubbles up and explodes. It is so intense. It is so great. It is meant to be shared. I have to share it with you, My precious child. I just have to. I can't keep it to Myself. It is too good to keep to Myself. My love bubbles up and out of Me unto all of Heaven and earth. My love is what matters more than anything in the entire universe.

"My child, receive My love for you. It is already pouring out and down from the heavens all over you. It was poured on the inside of you by precious Holy Spirit. My love is everywhere. Receive it. Don't be afraid to take it. Don't be afraid to ask for it. You were created for this extreme love. You were created for it. When I thought of you before the foundation of the world, I thought of pouring my love in you and on you, all over you. It brings Me so much joy to love on you. This is what you are here for. This is how you experience the abundant life. This is how you bear fruit. This is how you overcome temptations to sin. This is how you receive the victory. This is how you experience the fullness of My glory. When you know My love for you, which keeps you in My perfect peace, you are not easily deceived by the enemy's lies.

"My love conquers all. Beloved, do you have to battle fear all of the time? Precious one, you were not created to constantly battle a spirit of fear. You were created to receive My love and let My love destroy all fear in your life. When you know My love, fear has no place even in the trials. Child, know that your biggest destiny is to experience My love that bubbles up and out of Me over the entire universe, including you. Precious one, this is My gift to you. Will you receive it?"

1 John 4:16; Romans 5:5; 1 Corinthians 13:13; Ephesians 4:10

Prayer:

Heavenly Daddy, thank You for creating me to share Your love with. I am amazed at Your love and want a deeper revelation of it. I choose to believe by faith right now that You indeed love me with an everlasting love. In Jesus' name, Amen.

*Spend some time thanking Daddy for creating you so that He could love on you. Tell Him you want to feel His love pouring all over you today in a special way.

*Write a letter to your Daddy telling Him how you felt
when you read His love letter to you today.*

_____

_____

_____

_____

_____

_____

_____

_____

_____

_____

_____

_____

_____

_____

_____

_____

_____

_____

~Day 20~

I TREASURE THE WORDS YOU SPEAK TO ME

"My precious child, I want you to know that you are so valuable to Me. I have lots of children, and I cherish every single one of them. I even know the number of hairs on each of My children's heads, including yours. I know the color of your eyes. I know where every freckle is found on you. I know every intimate detail about all of My children. I know what words you will speak before a word is ever uttered. I know everything there is to know about you. I value and love you.

"Beloved, I want you to know that I value you so much that I treasure every word you speak to Me. I treasure every second that you fellowship with Me. When you tell Me that you love Me, it brings so much joy to My heart. I value the love that you give Me. I never force you to love Me so any loving words you speak to Me are more valuable then all the treasure stored up in Heaven. Your words are more valuable than any gold or precious stones. I am more interested in you than any treasure. In fact, you are My precious treasure. I store your loving words in My heart, and I never forget them.

"I look forward to our conversations. I want you to remember that you bring Me great joy and you matter to Me. I treasure every single word you speak to Me because you are My beloved child and I love you. What words will I store in My heart today from you, precious one? I can't wait to hear them!"

Luke 12:7; Psalm 139; Song of Solomon 4:9

Prayer:

Dear Heavenly Daddy, I will remember how much it means to You to have me tell You how I feel about You. Thank You for reminding me that I am valuable and I matter to You and You know every intimate detail of my life. You love me more than I could ever imagine and that brings me great joy. I can't wait to talk to You throughout the day. You will have many words to store in Your heart from me. In Jesus' name, Amen.

*Spend some time speaking to your Heavenly Daddy. He treasures the words you speak to Him.

Spend some time writing a letter to your Heavenly Daddy
telling Him all the things that you love about Him.
He also treasures your love letters to Him.

~Day 21~

LET ME PUT THE PIECES TOGETHER FOR YOU

As I was feeling some emotional pain one day, I told the Lord, "I feel so broken." Immediately, He showed me a picture of a bunch of puzzle pieces. There were pieces all over, and I was trying to put the pieces together to complete the puzzle, but I couldn't do it. I was frustrated thinking the puzzle was too hard, and I wanted to give up. Next, I saw Jesus sitting on the floor by the pieces, and He was picking a piece up, kissing it, and then placing the kissed pieces together and putting the puzzle together for me. Next, He said these words:

"My precious child, I can put all of the broken pieces of your life back together. Let Me help you. Let Me show you that I am continually putting things together for you. Let Me take your brokenness and make it into a beautiful masterpiece. There are no impossible situations for Me. I can take the biggest broken mess and put it all back together and make it even better. Don't ever give up hope. Let Me put the pieces of your life back together for you. Let Me do it. Give Me all the pieces to the puzzle that you are struggling to put together yourself. Give them to Me and let Me breathe My love into them and put the pieces where they belong.

"Child, yes, sometimes you have done things on your own and put the pieces where you wanted to put them instead of letting Me place them where they needed to be. Precious one, it's ok. Once you realize that you can't put the pieces of your life together alone without Me, that is when you will finally start receiving major breakthrough in your life. You won't understand what is going on until you see the entire masterpiece put together. Trust Me to make a beautiful masterpiece out of every situation in your life. Only I can do it.

"Child, don't believe any lies from the enemy that tell you, 'You blew it again. There is no way to put this mess together again.' Those are lies. The truth is that you are precious to Me and everything will be alright. Trust Me!"

Luke 1:37

Prayer:

Heavenly Daddy, thank You for reminding me that You are making a beautiful masterpiece out of every aspect of my life, even the pain. Help me to trust You when I don't see the full picture. I know that You see the big picture and You tell me to trust You. I put my life in Your hands. In Jesus' name, Amen.

*Picture Him helping you put some pieces of your life together right now.

Spend some time writing to Daddy about the pieces of the puzzle in your life that you need Him to put together for you. Start writing decrees of victory and break the lie that says, "There is no way to put this mess together again."

_____

_____

_____

_____

_____

_____

_____

_____

_____

_____

_____

_____

_____

_____

_____

_____

_____

_____

_____

_____

~Day 22~

PLEASE, DON'T FORGET ABOUT THE CROSS!

I saw a vision of Jesus, and He was weeping. I could hear Him say in a very sad voice, "Please, don't forget about the cross. Live as if the cross makes a difference in your life. Don't forget about the cross. Don't forget about the greatest love act that will ever be recorded. Please, don't forget all about the cross. Ask Me for a revelation of what it means for you to live in the New Covenant, and I will give it to you. Search deep into My Word and see what I bought for you with My own life. Please, don't forget about the cross. The cross is power! The cross is healing! The cross is victory over death! The cross is total forgiveness! The cross is total victory over trials! The cross is total rest for My children! The cross is joy unspeakable!!! The cross is grace! The cross is mercy! The cross is love! The cross is love! The cross is passionate, burning love! It will take you an eternity to discover what happened at the cross. Please, don't forget about the cross. Please, don't forget about the emotional pain, the physical torture, the death, and resurrection. Don't forget about it. Please, don't forget that I endured it all because of My deep love for you. Please, don't forget about the cross."

After these words, I saw a vision of Paul. As Paul was writing these words, "For I determined to know nothing among you except Jesus Christ, and him crucified" (1 Corinthians 2:2 NASB), Jesus was jumping up and down with joy. He couldn't contain the joy He was feeling. He said, "Now My children will never forget the cross and what I went through to bless them with every spiritual blessing." Next, I saw a vision of time going by, and Jesus was watching the earth and seeing that the cross was slowly being forgotten. His heart was grieved. He said, "Please, bring the cross back. Don't forget about the most powerful, loving act that will ever be recorded. Don't forget about the New Covenant I made with you with My own blood. I hold dear all of My precious children who do not forget the cross. When you understand the cross, you understand My love for you."

1 Corinthians 2:2

Prayer:

Dear Jesus, I hunger for more revelation about what happened to You at Calvary. Show me, Jesus! Give me a revelation of what You purchased for me. Give me a hunger to know You, and You crucified. Thank You for Your resurrection. May I receive a deeper revelation of your resurrection and all that it means for me right now. I deeply desire to tell others about the cross. Please show me, Jesus. Amen.

*Spend some time thanking Jesus for the cross.

Spend some time writing down what the cross means to you. Then, spend some time writing a letter to Daddy asking Him for more revelation.

~Day 23 ~

PLEASE, DON'T FORGET ABOUT THE CROSS! – PART 2

The Lord gave me another vision from His heart. I saw a picture of some archaeologists. They had hammers and chisels in their hands, and they were delicately tapping dirt in search of some fossils. Next, I saw a picture of a huge cross. I saw these same people. Instead of chiseling in the dirt, they were now hammering and chiseling delicately on the cross. The Lord showed me a picture of what the cross had on the inside. There were many, many hidden gifts inside. Some were big, some were small, some were huge, and some were ever so tiny. When some of the people had found a few presents, they said, "Well, that must be all there is. I'll stop digging and searching now," and they left. Then, I saw some other people who said, "I want to dig deeper and see if there is more." I saw Jesus watching the people who stayed. He was overjoyed at their hunger to search deeper. These people who stayed found many hidden, precious treasures and gifts. The more they hammered and chiseled ever so delicately, the more they found. The more they found, the more joy they felt. The more they found, the more they felt loved by Jesus. Jesus was overflowing with ecstasy as He watched them find more and more and more gifts. He was so pleased with their hunger to know more about Him and the cross.

I heard Jesus say, "Many of My children do not understand the hidden truths of the cross. They read the Scriptures about what took place that day, but it doesn't make a difference in their life. They don't ask Holy Spirit to give them deep revelation about what happened and what the cross means. They don't know that there is more because they don't search for more. I absolutely love it when My children dig deeper. I love it when they dig with excitement for the next revelation about the cross and wonder what they will find next. I love their hunger. There is always more. I am waiting to give My children more and more and more revelation about the cross. Do you want more revelation about what I finished for you? Get ready. Get ready for a joy explosion! Get ready to get blasted! You will never be the same. Do you want it? Do you really want it? If you really want it, I will give it to you, My precious child. Let Me show you My love and the precious inheritance I purchased for you with My blood. Child, this revelation will change your life and give you the breakthrough you have been longing for."

1 Corinthians 2:2; Proverbs 25:2

*Spend some time asking the Lord to fill you with a hunger for more revelation about Jesus and His finished work on the cross. Spend some time thanking Jesus for the cross. Lift up His precious name and feel His liquid love flowing unto you. Worship Him and adore Him.

Spend some time writing a letter to your Daddy telling Him what this vision means to you. Next, spend some time asking Daddy to give you personal revelation of 1 Corinthians 2:2.

~Day 24~

FORGIVENESS SETS YOU FREE!

"My dear child, the person you have a difficult time forgiving is the person I love. Beloved, your debt was canceled and your slate was wiped completely clean when Jesus paid the price for all of your sins. Let this truth sink in. When you know how much you have been forgiven, it will be easier for you to forgive others and release them from the debt you feel they owe you. When you let go of all bitterness and un-forgiveness towards others, you will feel like a heavy load was lifted. You will feel lighter. You will feel freer. You will feel more joy and peace. When you forgive others, it sets you free in more ways than you will ever know.

"Beloved, I know people have harmed you and caused you much pain. My heart ached when I saw what you went through. However, when you choose to continue to hold on to un-forgiveness, you will continue to carry that pain around. That pain continues to harm you and is an open door for the enemy to harass you. Precious one, close the door on all un-forgiveness. Release the heavy load you have been carrying. Picture yourself dumping it at the cross. All sin and pain was taken away at the cross. Jesus took it for you. Release it, and you will see big changes in your life when you let others off the hook the way I let you off when Jesus took your punishment. Let My grace for you extend to everyone in your life and set you free to love others."

Colossians 2:13-14; Luke 7:36-47; Matthew 5:23-24; 18:23-35; Ephesians 4:2-3

Prayer:

Heavenly Father, I realize I have been carrying a heavy load of un-forgiveness towards some people in my life. Please show me anyone I am still holding un-forgiveness towards. Father, I say that I am ready to release them all from the debt I feel they owe me. Thank You Father for forgiving me and for wiping my slate of sins completely free through Jesus. I repent for all un-forgiveness and resentment right now. I choose to close the door on it and forgive others as You have so freely forgiven me. Thank You for Your forgiveness. In Jesus' precious name, Amen.

*Spend some time in prayer forgiving anyone you are holding un-forgiveness towards. Keep praying until you feel the burden lifted and the peace that comes from getting rid of all un-forgiveness.

Spend some time writing down prayers of blessings over those people whom you have just forgiven. Ask Daddy to help you see these people through His eyes of love.

~Day 25~

THE SECRET PLACE DATE

I saw a vision of a woman in a coffee shop. She was anxiously awaiting the arrival of her good friend. She would look at her watch and smile as she anticipated having a good conversation with her friend. Next, I saw her friend arrive. They hugged and sat down and began to fellowship together.

Next, I saw this same woman in the coffee shop waiting for this same friend. Only this time, the friend never showed up. The woman waited and waited, and when she finally realized her friend was not coming, she became very sad and felt rejected.

Next, I saw these same two visions, but instead of seeing the woman, I saw Jesus, and He was waiting for one of His children. Put yourself in the pictures. He is waiting for you. I heard Him say these words:

"My precious children, I absolutely look forward to our times when it is just the two of us in the secret place. You know that feeling you feel when you are looking forward to a date with a loved one? Well, that is how I feel when I fellowship with you. I am always waiting for you. I so look forward to our secret place dates. Come! Come into the secret place now. I have something prepared just for you. Come and be alone with Me and let's pour our hearts out together. I have so much to tell you. Come, let's relax and spend time together. Let Me tell you how I feel about you. It is you that I am waiting for and looking forward to spending time with. Yes, it is you, My precious child.

"Come, come into the secret place. I am looking forward to our date together. I will never stand you up. I will always be there, waiting patiently for you to join Me. Come, be alone with Me. I love you, precious, beloved child of Mine."

Matthew 6:6

Prayer:

Jesus, thank You for reminding me how important it is for me to spend alone time with You in the secret place. It brings me so much joy that You enjoy spending time with me. Thank You for all the love words You speak over me when I am alone with You. I am running to the secret place now to be alone with My lover. Thank You for being so good to Me. In Your name, Amen.

*Show Jesus how much you love Him by writing His name on your calendar and telling Him that you have a date with Him. I see Him smiling now.

Write Jesus a love letter telling Him how much you want to put Him first in your schedule. Tell Him how much it means to you that He wants to spend time with you in the secret place.

_____

_____

_____

_____

_____

_____

_____

_____

_____

_____

_____

_____

_____

_____

_____

_____

_____

_____

_____

_____

_____

_____

~Day 26~

I KISS MY BRIDE

I saw a vision of a Christian woman struggling with many addictions, feeling hopeless. She looked worn out and lifeless as she went to a church hoping to find freedom, but instead, the person at the pulpit was preaching shame and condemnation. In the Spirit, I saw a big huge whip beat her over her head. She felt like she had just been whipped. I saw her heart break as it felt even more pain and hopelessness than when she had entered the church. I knew in the vision that she didn't have a revelation of her identity and of what Jesus purchased for her on the cross. She was hopeless.

Next, I saw a vision of Jesus being whipped and beaten. He then went to the woman and was weeping as He cradled her in His arms and said, "No, this is not My heart towards you. I am love. I was beaten so that you could have a clear conscience. I took your sin and gave you My righteousness." I then saw a vision of Jesus' shed blood sprinkling the woman's conscience. "I was brutally crushed for all of your addictions." Then, in the Spirit, I saw a huge pile of alcohol bottles and needles. Like a magnet, they were drawn to the foot of the cross. I saw Jesus as He became sin. He was suffering. He looked very disfigured and worn out. He said, "This woman does not need to be beaten with guilt and shame, she needs love. My heart breaks for her. She already knows that what she is doing is wrong, but she wants freedom. She needs love, not to feel like she was whipped. I do not beat My bride up with guilt and shame. She needs to know that even when she is under the influence, I do not abandon her. No, I pursue her even more with My love and grace. Where there is sin, grace abounds. She needs to know that My blood has washed her completely clean, and, when she weeps with hopelessness, I wipe away her tears, and I whisper in her ear how much I love her and want her to be free. She needs to know I have already made her a new creation in Me and have given her authority over all the power of the enemy. She needs to know that she is My bride that will never be separated from My powerful, healing love. I do not whip My bride, rather I love on her. I kiss My bride, I do not whip her."

Next, I saw a vision of this same woman. This time, she went into a church where she heard a message on Jesus' love and His finished work. The message made the woman fall madly in love with Jesus. She also felt His passionate love for her. The walls in her life started to crumble. For the first time, the woman felt peace and love instead of shame and guilt. She felt Holy Sprit's liquid love warming her instead of alcohol and drugs. Her whole countenance changed. She said, "This is what I have been searching for."

Day 26 ~ I Kiss My Bride

Then the Lord said: "This is My heart of love. Please bring the love message of the cross back to My people so that they can be free."

Psalm 103:3-4; Hebrews 9:13-14; 10:10; Romans 5:20; 6:14; Isaiah 1:18

Prayer:

Jesus, this picture is so touching to me. Thank You for reminding me that Your heart is love and not guilt and condemnation. Thank You for showing me that the way to freedom is to understand what is already mine, not to be reminded about my failures, which only bring more shame, guilt and sin. Help me to share with others the truly good news of the gospel, Your undeserved favor. Help me to also extend myself love and grace when I fail, because that is what You do for me. In Your name, Amen.

*Spend some time praying. Afterwards, picture Jesus kissing you, even when you sin. Let this truth help you fall deeper in love with Him and set you free.

Write down how it makes you feel that Jesus wants to kiss you with His love.

~Day 27~

YOU ARE MY TREASURE!

I saw a touching vision. I saw a huge treasure chest in Heaven. I saw the arms of our Heavenly Daddy open the treasure chest. When He opened it, all of His children were in there. He said this:

"You are My precious treasure. I treasure every single one of My children. I am so grieved when people don't make it into this treasure chest. I pursue everybody to come into My treasure chest, but many reject Me. That saddens Me beyond words. However, when I look into the treasure chest and see who wanted to be with Me forever, I am filled with such joy and bliss.

"Never forget how I feel about you. You need to be reminded daily about My love for you. This is a revelation the enemy continually wants to steal from you. I even want you to write or print out Scriptures that talk about My love for you, and I want you to meditate on them. Ask precious Holy Spirit to open your eyes to see the truth of what these words mean. Holy Spirit loves to be involved in your life. He loves it when you ask Him to reveal the Word to you. Ask Him for revelation as you meditate on these truths.

"The enemy tells you, 'You are not worthy to be in the presence of the Lord because of what you just did.' I tell you, 'You are My cherished treasure that I value so much. I hold the lock and the key and no one can take you out of this chest, out of My possession.' The enemy tells you, 'What did you do today to earn God's love? You didn't work hard enough.' I tell you over and over, 'My love to you is a gift. It is your treasure. You don't have to do anything to earn My love for you. You already possess it!'

"Child, don't just view yourself as My child. View yourself as My precious, valuable treasure that I love to admire and take care of because that is the truth."

Deuteronomy 7:6; John 14:26

Prayer:

Heavenly Daddy, thank You for choosing me before the foundation of the world to be Your precious treasure. I feel so overwhelmed with joy to think of spending eternity in Your Kingdom with You. I treasure being Your child. In Jesus' name, Amen.

*Keep reminding yourself throughout the day that you are Daddy's treasure and that you don't need to earn His love; it is a gift. Give Him glory and praise Him.

Write down several times, "I am My Heavenly Daddy's treasure forever." Spend some time writing down what this means to you. If you don't feel like His treasure, write down how you want this revelation in your life.

_____

_____

_____

_____

_____

_____

_____

_____

_____

_____

_____

_____

_____

_____

_____

_____

_____

_____

_____

_____

~Day 28~

MY SON SAT DOWN SO THAT YOU CAN REST

"My beloved, you were completely cleansed by the blood of Jesus the moment you accepted Him as your Savior. However, I know the enemy continually reminds you of your sins and your past. Yet, I tell you to renew your mind with the truth that you have been washed white as snow by His blood. Let this truth annihilate any guilt and shame you feel about any sins you have committed or future ones.

"In the Old Testament, the high priests stood all day offering sacrifices on behalf of the people. In spite of all of the sacrifices, their sins were only covered. However, the shed blood of Jesus on the cross completely cleansed you from all past, present, and future sins. My Son SAT DOWN at My right hand when He finished removing your sins as far as the East is from the West. He sat down to show you that He was the final sacrifice, the final punishment for all of your sins.

"My beloved, because My Son sat down, you can now rest your conscience. Get rid of all self-condemnation, guilt, and shame. Instead, rest in the good news that I see you as white as snow, without a single fault before Me. Let this truth set you free to live a holy life. This is truly the good news. Because of Christ's finished work on the cross, you can now sit and rest in My unending, unconditional love for you."

Hebrews 1:3; Titus 3:5; Isaiah 1:18; Psalm 103:12; Hebrews 10:11-12; 12:2; 7:27; 4:9; Colossians 1:22

Prayer:

Heavenly Daddy, help me to remember the good news that You see me white as snow before You without a single fault. Help me to ward off all the lies of the enemy that tell me the opposite of this truth. I choose to get rid of all self-condemnation, guilt, and shame right now in the name of Jesus. Help me to receive Your love. Give me a deeper revelation of who I am in Christ. Show me my true identity. Thank You Jesus for not just covering my sins, but taking them away and removing them forever. This truth makes me fall deeper in love with You rather than making me want to go out and sin. To You be all glory, honor, and praise. In Your precious name, Amen.

*Keep reminding yourself today that you have been washed white as snow because of the finished work of Christ. Thank Jesus for making you clean.

Read Hebrews 10 and write down your thoughts on it.
Journal about any verses that Holy Spirit highlights to you.

~Day 29~

HEALING BELONGS TO MY CHILDREN

"Precious child, it overwhelms Me with sadness when My children think that I would ever put sickness on them to teach them a lesson. It grieves Me when My children believe that I pick and choose who I heal or don't heal. It saddens Me when My children think that they don't qualify for healing and that I am withholding it from them.

"My beloved precious child, I never, ever put sickness on My children. The truth is that My Son took all of your sicknesses on the cross the day He was brutally tortured and tormented. Oh, how I long for all of My children to get the revelation that Jesus paid for their total and complete healing on the cross! When He said, 'It is finished!' He meant, 'Sickness is finished!' Healing is available to ALL of My children, every single one of them.

"The enemy comes to steal, kill, and destroy. He loves to destroy My children with sickness. However, My Son gave you total authority over all the power of the enemy. The enemy was crushed and defeated by Jesus. Child, read about this in My Word and get this revelation. All the answers to healing are in My Word. Beloved, ask Me for revelation that by Jesus' stripes, you WERE healed. Let Me show you this. He did this all for His deep, powerful love for you. I sent My Son to give you an abundant life, not a life filled with sickness and disease. It grieves Me to see you suffer.

"I have plans to prosper you and not to harm you. Don't let anyone make you believe that I want you to suffer with sickness. This is a lie from the pit of hell! When the leper asked My Son if He was willing to heal him, My Son did not hesitate, and He said, "Yes, I am willing." He did this to show that My will is always for My children to be healed. Let this truth sink deep into your heart. Healing is a finished work of the cross and a gift that belongs to all of My children. I love you and want you to receive this gift. It is your inheritance."

Isaiah 53:5; Galatians 3:13; John 10:10; Luke 10:19; Colossians 2:15; Jeremiah 29:11; Mark 1:40-42

Prayer: Heavenly Father, thank You for showing me that Jesus already purchased my healing. Give me the revelation that healing is my inheritance and that You are not withholding anything from me. In Jesus' name, Amen.

*Picture any sickness you are struggling with on Jesus' body on the cross because He took it from you that day.

Spend some time writing a letter to Jesus thanking Him for taking the curse of sickness on the cross and for purchasing your healing. If you are struggling with any sickness or disease, write down, "Jesus took _____ on the cross for me. Healing is mine, and I am taking it back. By Jesus' stripes, I am healed."

~Day 30~

I AM YOUR DADDY, HUSBAND, AND FRIEND!

"My child, My bride, and My friend, I want you to know that I am all you need. I am your Daddy, your husband, and your friend. I am all that you need. Come to Me and let Me fill every void in your life. I want to take care of all your needs. Let Me take care of you. Let Me carry you through life. Let Me carry you through all of your trials. Let Me provide for all of your needs. What do you need? Come into the secret place and tell Me now. I am listening, My beloved.

"You are my precious creation. I created you to depend on Me. When you fully depend on Me for all of your needs, you will truly experience the abundant life you were created to live. When you realize that I am all you need, you will feel true, everlasting peace. When you rest and melt in My arms, you will receive supernatural provision for all of your needs. When you are striving to depend on yourself, I can't help you the way that I would like to. I let you do things your own way until you realize that you need Me. The enemy likes to feed you lies that you can handle everything on your own. The kingdom of darkness tries to separate us and tries to make you think that I am distant, uninterested in you, and I am not taking care of you. Those are lies from the pit! You have my undivided attention 24 hours a day! I am always with you, listening to you, whispering to you, guiding you, and holding you. I want to take care of your every need, and I care about every desire of your heart.

"Beloved, I want you to know Me as your Daddy, your husband, and your friend. There is intimacy in a Daddy/child relationship. There is intimacy in a husband/wife relationship. And there is intimacy in a friend relationship. I want to be the most intimate relationship in your life. When I am the most intimate relationship in your life, you are so filled with My glory that everybody around you notices Me in you, and people are drawn to you. My glory in you will transform the world around you. Come, let Me be everything to you, and you will never, ever lack anything."

1 John 3:1; Jeremiah 31:32; Hosea 2:16; John 15:15; Isaiah 54:5

Prayer:

Heavenly Daddy, I want a deeper relationship with You. I'm sorry that I sometimes doubt that You will meet my every need, but the more I know the love You have for me, the more I can stand against this lie from the enemy. I truly desire You to be the most intimate relationship in my life. In Jesus' name, Amen.

Spend some time writing your Heavenly Daddy a love letter telling Him why He is all you need. Tell Him that you want to know Him as your Daddy, Husband, and Friend.

~Day 31~

MY BLAZING EYES OF FIRE ARE FULL OF PASSIONATE LOVE FOR YOU!

"Child, My blazing eyes of fire gaze into your eyes with a burning, passionate love that I want you to know and receive.

"Beloved, this passionate love for you never, ever fades or goes out. You cannot cause these flaming eyes of love for you to be extinguished. Precious one, you are worthy to receive this burning, passionate, unconditional, everlasting love from Me. I cannot remind you enough that you were created to receive this love.

"When you get a glimpse of the passionate love I have for you, you will be completely transformed from the inside out. You will feel peace, love, and joy on the inside, and this will flow out to others. It will naturally flow out of you. You won't have to work to feel peace on the inside; it will naturally happen. I cannot remind you enough how much I love you. Receiving My passionate love for you is the key to absolutely everything. It is the key to breakthrough. It is the key to power in your life. It is the key to walking in the miraculous. It is the key to peace in your relationships and family. It truly is the key to receiving your inheritance because, when you know how much I love you, you truly believe that I do have a rich inheritance for you to receive right now. When you get a revelation of this love, it will destroy all fear that has been attacking you because you will have faith to believe that I am for you and not against you and that I meet all of your needs."

Revelation 19:12; Jeremiah 31:3; Ephesians 3:17-19

Prayer:

Heavenly Daddy, it is so hard for me to grasp sometimes how much You dearly love me. I know it is the key to complete breakthrough in my life. Thank You for continuing to renew my mind with the truth that You love me with a passionate, everlasting love forever. Father, let me feel Your passionate love at this very moment. Let it flow from me today unto others that I meet or talk to. Give me Your eyes to see how You love others in my life as well. Let me sense Your loving, blazing eyes of fire gazing at me today. In Jesus' name, Amen.

Spend some time writing a letter to Jesus thanking Him that He loves you with a passionate, burning love like no other. Keep thanking Him until you feel His love burning for you.

_____

_____

_____

_____

_____

_____

_____

_____

_____

_____

_____

_____

_____

_____

_____

_____

_____

_____

_____

_____

_____

_____

~Day 32~

YOU ARE THE BEAUTIFUL PEARL I CAME TO GET

I saw a vision of Jesus. He was on a mission. He was traveling, and He had all kinds of equipment with Him on His back to help him travel across the different types of terrain. I saw Him walking many, many miles. I saw Him walking on dirt paths. I saw Him walking in snow. The whole time He was traveling, He was focused on His mission. Whenever He made it through an area, He would leave behind the equipment He used for it. Finally, when He had reached the ocean, He had nothing left except scuba gear. I saw Him put it on and then go into the ocean. I even saw Him go through ocean caves and tight places in order to get to where He needed to be. Finally, I saw Him dive down deep in the water. He picked up what He came to get and came back to the surface of the water and then to dry land. I saw Him. He was smiling. He had retrieved an oyster. I saw Him open the oyster and inside was a beautiful pearl. He smiled. He was ecstatic. He took it out, discarded its outer shell, and washed it off until it was shiny, perfectly white, and beautiful. I then saw Him go up into Heaven, and He placed the beautiful pearl in a treasure chest and He said these words:

"You are the beautiful pearl I came to get. I had you on My mind when I came to the earth as a man. I had you on My mind when I traveled the earth and eventually went to the cross. You never left My thoughts. I would do it all again just for you. You were worth every single lash. You were worth all of the exhaustion. You were worth the pain. You were worth the agony. You were worth it.

"Child, the shell coming off of the pearl represents Me taking your old man on the cross and making you a new, beautiful, clean pearl. Precious one, just as I washed off the pearl in the vision, I have also washed you white as snow. That was part of My mission—to find you, to save you, to make you a new creation, to set you free, to wash you clean, and to seat you in Heavenly places. Because of what I have done for you, I now see you brightly shining before Me. Beloved, you couldn't wash yourself clean. I had to do it. Only I could make you clean and beautiful.

"My bride, you would be lost forever without Me. If I didn't come to get that pearl, it would be lost in the ocean forever surrounded by the outer shell in darkness. However, I had a mission to come and get that oyster to make it a beautiful treasure. I brought that beautiful treasure (you) into My Kingdom to be with Me forever. I value each and every one of My treasures. You are all like precious pearls to Me. I want you to know who you really are and how valuable you are to Me. I want you to see that you were worth the mission. I became nothing and emptied Myself for you. You were worth it. Come into the secret place and let Me show you.

Day 32 ~ You Are the Beautiful Pearl I Came to Get

Matthew 13:46; 2 Corinthians 5:17; Isaiah 1:18; Colossians 1:13

Prayer:

Jesus, thank You for coming to get me, to save me, to wash me clean, and to make me a new creation. I am in awe that You love me that much. Help this passionate love sink in. It overwhelms me to think that You also view me as a special treasure in Your Kingdom. I also want You to know that I view You as my special treasure that I can't wait to spend eternity with. In Your name, Amen.

*Today, think about what Jesus went through to go to the cross and take your cup of wrath. Remind yourself over and over, "I am my Daddy's special treasure. He sent Jesus to come and get me, wash me clean, and make me a new creation."

Write down what this vision means to you personally.

_____
_____
_____
_____
_____
_____
_____
_____
_____
_____
_____
_____
_____
_____
_____
_____
_____
_____

~Day 33~

I HEAR YOU EVERY TIME YOU CRY OUT TO ME

I saw a vision of a woman who was in extreme emotional pain. She fell on the floor in her room and started crying out to Jesus. She cried, "I don't think I can make it another day." I saw a vision of Jesus in Heaven. When He heard her cry out, He looked at everyone in Heaven and said, "Stop! My bride is crying out to Me." When He said, "Stop!" I saw that everything became motionless. He then went down to His bride, picked her up in His arms, and cradled her. He kept whispering in her ear, "I love you, My precious bride. I love you. I'm here. I hear you. Things are already happening in the spiritual realm to help you and bring you your victory. Don't give up hope, My bride. Don't give up hope. Put your hope in Me." Jesus then went back to Heaven and everything went back to normal. I heard these words:

"Beloved, I want you to get the full revelation that when you cry out to Me, it's as if nothing else matters to Me. You have My full, undivided attention. I hear your every cry, and I immediately come to comfort you. You are so precious to Me and everything that you care about, I care about. Everything. My desire is for you to receive your victory in every situation. I desire for you to come to Me for answers. I desire for you to trust that I am always for you. I want you to believe that I am working things out for your good. I want you to continue to cry out to Me, and I will show you incredible things you do not know. Keep crying out to Me. There is healing when you call on Me. There is comfort when you call on Me. There is peace when you call on Me. There is intimacy between us when you call on Me. Never stop crying out to Me and never stop believing that I hear you and I will answer you every single time. I tell you everything will be alright.

"You are so incredibly precious to Me. I am always with you. I will never, ever leave you. Know that when you call on Me in the secret place, the protection of My wings around you tightens the grip. Know that I am protecting you and loving on you, and I will never stop. Wait on Me, and I will give you strength."

Jeremiah 33:3; Romans 8:28; Psalm 91:4, 15; Isaiah 40:31

Prayer:

Heavenly Daddy, thank You so much for this touching picture. Thank You for showing me that You care about everything that matters to me especially when I cry out to You. Thank You for comforting me and for showing me Your love and for reassuring me that everything will be alright. In Jesus' name, Amen.

Write down what this vision means to you. Afterwards, spend some time praising Jesus for His incredible love and attention.

_____

_____

_____

_____

_____

_____

_____

_____

_____

_____

_____

_____

_____

_____

_____

_____

_____

_____

_____

~Day 34~

YOU HAVE ROYAL AUTHORITY

"Child, I want you to drown out any voice that tells you that you are not worthy. Ignore any voice that tells you that you don't deserve My love, blessings, and favor. Those are the voices of the enemy trying to deceive you. He wants to rob you of your royal inheritance that My Son bought for you. The enemy wants to bring you into self-pity and self-condemnation. He knows that you are royalty and have a mighty inheritance. He knows that when you get a hold of this truth, you will be walking around like royalty, destroying his powerless kingdom.

"You are a child of the King of Kings and a joint heir with Christ. The truth is that you have My favor with you wherever you go, whether you realize it or not, because Christ lives in you. My favor and blessings are all over you, and I want this truth to be unveiled to you. When you understand that you are royalty and Royalty lives in you, your life will change. Child, this day, picture yourself with a crown on your head and a scepter in your hand because you ARE royalty!

"You belong to My Kingdom, which has total authority over the kingdom of darkness. I have given you authority to trample over the enemy who was defeated at the cross. When he comes to tempt you or harass you or lie to you, use the authority I have given you to tell him to beat it and leave you alone. The only power he has over you is the power that you let him have. He was stripped of his power when My Son crushed him at Calvary. If you do not understand the authority I have given you, you won't use it and will remain powerless. Beloved, I tell you to use the authority that you have as a royal child in My Kingdom against the kingdom of darkness. I have given you authority to destroy the works of the devil. His kingdom is under your feet. I tell you to stamp your feet now to remind yourself that I have given you the authority to trample all over him any time he comes after you. He is defeated and powerless, yet the same power that raised Christ from the dead lives in you! This is good news!"

1 Peter 2:9; Romans 8:17; Ephesians 1:10-11, 13-14; Luke 10:19; Romans 8:11; Psalm 90:13

Prayer:

Heavenly Father, thank You for making me a part of Your Heavenly Kingdom and showing me all that belongs to me. Help me to remember to use the authority that You have given me over the enemy in order to experience my inheritance of total freedom. Remind me that I am royalty in Your eyes. In Jesus' name, Amen.

Meditate on some verses talking about your authority.
Spend some time writing them down and what they mean to you.

_____
_____
_____
_____
_____
_____
_____
_____
_____
_____
_____
_____
_____
_____
_____
_____
_____
_____
_____
_____

~Day 35~

JESUS: NAME ABOVE ALL NAMES!

I saw a vision. I saw a picture of Jesus' arms reaching up high above His head. I did not see His head in the vision. I saw His arms raised high and He was holding a sign that said, "JESUS." I saw words underneath the word JESUS. Here are some of the words I saw: fear, stress, death, sickness, mental illness, cancer, alcoholism, overeating, anger, and loneliness. The list was so long that I could not see the whole thing. I heard the Lord say, "The name of Jesus is above all names. It is also above all sickness, addiction, pain, and destruction. There is nothing too big for the name of Jesus to conquer. There is nothing that is impossible in the name of Jesus. There is no medical diagnosis bigger than the name of Jesus. There is no addiction too hard for the name of Jesus. There is total and complete victory in the name of Jesus."

Next, I saw the name of Jesus fall and crush the long list to the ground, and I heard the Lord say, "Child, I want you to focus on all that Jesus is and all that He did for you. I want you to see that, because of the cross, total victory is possible in your life, total freedom is possible in your life, total peace is possible in your life, and total healing is possible in your life. My Son crushed everything that came in with the evil one because of His great, extreme love for you. Beloved, realize that I want you to be completely set free from all the chains that are binding you. Complete freedom is your inheritance. Receive it! I came to set the captives free! Be free to experience the abundant life. I am not withholding. Child, come to Me and let Me set you totally and completely free. Let Me renew your mind with My loving words. Come, I have some things to show you. I am waiting, My beloved."

Philippians 2:9-11; Isaiah 53:5; 61:1; John 8:36; 10:10; Ephesians 1:20-21

Prayer:

Heavenly Father, thank You for reminding me that Jesus came to set me free from absolutely everything that keeps me from experiencing the abundant life He died to give me. Father, I pray for more revelation that freedom is mine because Jesus bought if for me with His blood. Show me what needs to go in my life. May I receive a revelation of Your deep love so that I can be free. In Jesus' name, Amen.

*Spend some time exalting the name of Jesus.

Day 35 ~ Jesus: Name Above All Names!

Spend some time writing down whatever you are struggling with.
Next, write down, "The name of Jesus is above ________________.
There is victory in the name of Jesus."

~Day 36~

I LOVE IT WHEN YOU GLORIFY JESUS!

"Beloved, oh, how it brings Me great joy when you lift up the name of Jesus! I love it when you praise His precious name! My Son deserves all glory, honor, and praise!

"There are treasures in the name of Jesus. Beloved, there is healing and deliverance. There is joy and peace. There is everlasting love in the name of Jesus. There is victory in the name of Jesus. There is freedom in the name of Jesus. Lift His name high above every other name! Praise Him! Glorify Him! Tell Him how much you appreciate Him sacrificing His life and becoming your sin. Tell Him how grateful you are that He took your punishment. Tell Him how much you love and adore Him.

"I am filled with joy when you glorify My precious Son. You will be filled with joy, peace, and love when you praise His holy name. Praise Him and watch your circumstances change. Praise Him and watch temptations flee. Praise Him and see the enemy scatter. Praise Him and watch your countenance change before your very eyes. Praise Him and others around you will notice the glory on your face. My treasure, you cannot help but be blessed and completely transformed when you glorify Jesus. When you praise Him, adore Him, behold Him, your life will be transformed without striving. His glory will be all over you. Your light will shine brightly wherever you go, and you will experience incessant, contagious joy! Praise the name of Jesus! He is so worthy to be praised and adored!"

John 14:27; Galatians 5:1; Luke 10:19; Philippians 2:9

Prayer:

Father, I am making a commitment to glorify Jesus in a special way today. Help me to remember to praise His holy name wherever I go and whatever I do. Please show me Jesus in a deeper way. Jesus, I lift Your name above all names and say that You are so worthy to be praised, glorified, loved, and adored. Thank You for giving me Your righteousness in exchange for my sin. You are so worthy to be praised and adored! Thank You for the joy I feel even now as I say Your precious name. In Your holy name, Amen.

*Spend some time worshiping Jesus and lifting up His name. Read about Him in the Scriptures and ask Him to touch you with a personal word. Praise Him and give Him glory whenever you can throughout the day.

Spend some time writing down praises to Jesus from your heart.

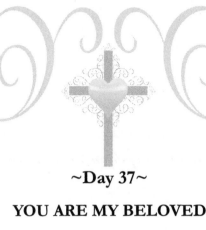

~Day 37~

YOU ARE MY BELOVED

"Dear precious child, I want you to know that you are My beloved. I cherish you! I chose you before the foundation of the world to be My child. I rejoiced the day you were born, and I was even with you while you were in your mother's womb. You are not a mistake! You were perfectly planned to be here. I planned to spend eternity with you from the moment I thought of you.

"Child, you are My beloved, and I have a destiny for you. The enemy sometimes deceives you into not knowing how much I cherish you. He also deceives you into thinking that I don't have great plans for you. Those are lies from the lying kingdom of darkness. I tell you that I have a huge destiny for you because you are My beloved child.

"When you look into the mirror, I want you to see yourself the way I see you. I want you to tell yourself, 'I am Daddy's beloved, and He adores me just the way I am.' Remind yourself that I adore you all the time. Remind yourself that you are precious to Me. When I look at you, I am so elated with what I see that my heart skips a beat. Beloved, realize that I am so proud of you, and I am overjoyed that you belong to Me. When I think about you, I smile with bliss! Please do not forget that you bring Me much happiness. I am so happy to be your Heavenly Daddy! You are truly My beloved!"

Matthew 17:5; John 15:16; Ephesians 1:5

Prayer:

My Heavenly Daddy, please help me to see more and more that I truly am Your beloved child. Help me to see how precious I am to You so that my life can be transformed and radically changed by Your love and grace. Knowing how much You love me causes me to fall even deeper in love with You, and it helps me to resist the temptations of the enemy. So Father, give me a deeper revelation of the love You have for me. Thank You for choosing me to be Your child. In Jesus' name, Amen!

*Spend time throughout the day saying, "I am my Heavenly Daddy's beloved child. If He is for me, who can be against me? I am His precious child."

*Spend some time journaling what it means to you to be
your Heavenly Daddy's beloved child.*

~Day 38~

I LOVE IT WHEN YOU SAY "GOOD MORNING" TO ME

"My precious child, I love it when you wake up and the first thing you do is acknowledge My presence with you. Holy Spirit whispers to you, 'Good morning, My beloved,' the moment you awaken. If you start your day saying, 'Good morning, Holy Spirit,' your whole attitude about the day will change for the better.

"When you acknowledge that I am with you and in you first thing in the morning, you can't help but be filled with faith. I will remind you that you can do all things because My Son in you is strengthening you and giving you daily supernatural energy to achieve what you need to do.

"When you acknowledge Me in the morning, you open up opportunities to hear My voice and converse throughout the day. I love it when we talk together. I want to fill you with My loving words before you start your day. I want you to be filled with My love the moment you awaken to help you with any trials that come your way in the day.

"Beloved, if you start your day with 'Good morning' to Me, you will be abundantly blessed. It fills Me with such bliss when My precious ones have an intimate relationship with Me and acknowledge Me in the morning the same way that they would their loved ones.

"Dear one, give it a try, and you will see changes in our relationship and intimacy."

Philippians 4:13

Prayer:

Heavenly Daddy, help me to acknowledge Your presence with me the moment I awaken. The desire of my heart is deeper intimacy with You. Help me to hear precious Holy Spirit whispering "Good morning" and speaking to me throughout the day. Thank You for Your fellowship. You are precious to me. In Jesus' name, Amen.

*This week, commit to acknowledging Holy Spirit first thing in the morning and be blessed. First thing in the morning, tell Holy Spirit how happy you are that He is with you and desires intimacy with you. Tell Him that you are excited to spend the day with Him and look forward to all He has for you.

Spend some time writing down what it means to you
that Holy Spirit speaks to you the moment you awaken.

_____
_____
_____
_____
_____
_____
_____
_____
_____
_____
_____
_____
_____
_____
_____
_____
_____
_____
_____

~Day 39~

GET TO KNOW HOLY SPIRIT INTIMATELY

"Child, precious Holy Spirit is a person, and He is My cherished gift to you and all My children who want Him. He is part of Me! He is longing for you to get to know Him, to fellowship with Him, and to make Him a part of your life. He wants to be your closest friend. He is your comforter, your teacher, your guide, your friend, and so much more. Holy Spirit is patient. He doesn't force you to acknowledge His presence, but oh, how He is so excited when you get a revelation that He is with you, talking to you, giving you ideas, telling you about what Jesus did for you! He also wants to help you pray. Sometimes you don't know how to pray, but ask Him to help you, and He will help you. He loves to help you. He loves to be with you. He loves you to pieces, and He wants you to talk to Him.

"Precious one, ask Him questions. Get to know Holy Spirit intimately. Ask Him what He likes, and He will show you. Ask Him what grieves Him, and He will show you. Acknowledge His presence in you. He adores you, and He cherishes fellowship with you. He is longing and waiting for intimate relationship with all of My children. Child, will you get to know Him? He is patiently waiting. He adores you and wants to reveal Jesus to you in a new way. He also wants to share secrets with you. Will you let Him? He is My gift to you while you are here on the earth so that you will never, ever be alone. Invite Him to fellowship with you. He feels loved and honored when you do this.

"Get to know precious Holy Spirit intimately! You will be filled to the overflow with joy and peace when you get to know Him and feel His presence with you. He is My gift to you!"

John 14:16-17; John 16:6-7, 13-15

Prayer:

Heavenly Daddy, thank You so much for Your gift of Holy Spirit. I am going to get to know Him in a new way today by asking Him questions and spending time with Him. Thank You for reminding me that Holy Spirit wants to reveal Jesus in a deeper way in my life. I am going to ask Him to reveal Jesus to me even today. Amen.

*Spend some special time praying in the Spirit.

Spend some time writing down a thank you letter to Holy Spirit for being with you and wanting relationship with you. Write to Him of how you want to know Him more. Tell Holy Spirit how you feel about Him until you feel His presence.

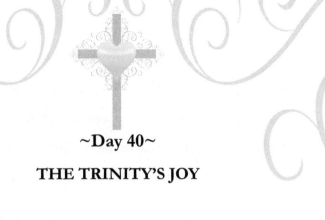

~Day 40~

THE TRINITY'S JOY

I saw a vision of Holy Spirit. He was whispering revelations of Jesus to God's children. I saw that many people weren't listening and didn't hear anything, and Holy Spirit was grieved. Then, I saw that the ones who listened, who heard, their faces lit up, and they started to weep in gratitude to Jesus. Holy Spirit was ecstatic. I heard those people thanking the Father for sending Jesus. I saw them thanking Jesus for enduring the cross and taking their punishment, for setting them free, and for giving them joy. Next, I heard the Father and Jesus weeping with joy. Their hearts were deeply touched. Then, I saw the Father's hands reach down from Heaven and gather up in His hands all of those who were worshiping with gratitude. He brought them up to the surface of Heaven, and His tears were falling on them. The people were touched, and they were completely transformed and blasted by His love. They could not stand. They just soaked up His love, and then He put them back down. It was a very touching scene. Next, I heard these words:

"My beloved children, when you receive the revelation of all that Jesus is, all that Jesus did, and all that Jesus means, I am so touched. I am so touched when you are filled with gratitude and you start thanking My Son for what He did. When you do this, you understand the reason you are here. You understand love. You start to understand My loving kindness for you, and that is what leads you to true repentance and freedom. Beloved, nothing touches My heart more than when you worship Jesus and glorify Jesus. My Son is high and lifted up. My Son deserves all the honor and glory. My Son did it all for you. When you lift up His name, your heart will be touched with My love for you. When you understand the love of My Son, you are forever changed. You are forever changed with a joy and peace that surpasses all understanding.

"Precious one, do you hear Holy Spirit's whispers telling you about My Son? Listen quietly. Go to the secret place now and be touched with the greatest love that ever existed."

Romans 2:4; Revelation 5:12; John 3:14-15; Ephesians 3:17-19

Prayer:

Heavenly Daddy, thank You for this touching vision. Thank You for giving me the gift of precious Holy Spirit who continues to give me revelation about Jesus. May I never stop receiving the revelation You want to impart to me. You are so precious to me. In Jesus' name, Amen.

*Spend some time loving on Father, Jesus, and Holy Spirit.

Write down what this vision means to you personally.

~Day 41~

LOOK UP, NOT DOWN

"Beloved, the enemy wants you to look down and not up. Precious child, don't ever look down in shame. The enemy wants to keep you in shame. I know he tells you things like, 'You should be bearing more fruit by now. You are a horrible Christian because you find it hard to love others.' He tells you lies to keep you looking down in shame and not up at My face. Child, look up. Look at Me. I want to see your precious face. I want to gaze into your beautiful eyes. I am never ashamed of you. I love you so much. You are so precious and beautiful to Me. Receive the truth that I absolutely adore you and you are My precious bride. Child, look up at My face. Let My glory radiate onto you. Look up at My face and let My eyes of love melt your heart. Look up at My face and let My eyes of love take all shame away. Look up, not down.

"Child, when you look down, the enemy wins. He wants you to focus on all your struggles and every single sin you still struggle with. Child, when you look down and focus on your sins, it only makes you feel more shame and guilt and makes you want to sin even more. When you focus on sin, you do not focus on Me, and you do not focus on the righteousness that I gave you at the cross. Child, stop focusing on your sins and start looking up. Start looking at My face and focus on My love for you. Focus on My glory. Focus on Me as your healer. Focus on Me as your husband. Focus on Me as your deliverer. I am all these and so much more. The more you seek My face, the more glory you will experience. The more you seek My face, the more victory you will have in your life. The more you seek My face, the more spiritual fruit you will bear without effort. In order to seek My face, you need to look up and not down.

"Precious one, get rid of all of the shame. Shame comes from the kingdom of darkness. I took it upon Myself at the cross so that you wouldn't have to live with it. I did not create you to feel shame. I created you to feel loved by Me. When you feel loved by Me, shame has no place to stay anymore. Come, let Me love you right now. Come, look up into My eyes of love. I'm waiting!"

1 Corinthians 15:56; Romans 8:1; 2 Corinthians 5:21

Prayer:

Jesus, thank You for reminding me that You took all of my shame on the cross. Thank You for reminding me that I am worthy to look at You and seek Your face even when I sin because You still see me as righteous in Your sight. I close the door on all shame right now. Holy Spirit, come and fill me with the love of Jesus. In Your name, Amen.

Spend some time writing down what the words in today's devotional mean to you personally. Share your heart with Daddy.

_____

_____

_____

_____

_____

_____

_____

_____

_____

_____

_____

_____

_____

_____

_____

_____

_____

~Day 42~

MY BANNER OVER YOU IS LOVE

I was at a soccer game. In the stadium, I could see many fans waving banners in support of their team. People were really excited about the game. People were shouting and blowing horns. Excitement was in the air. The Lord began to speak to me about what was on His heart. He said, "Oh, how I wish all of My children would be this excited about Me being their Daddy." I could feel the pain in His heart for the lost. I could also feel that He was grieved that many of His children do not have an intimate relationship with Him and are more excited about the things of this world than they are about having a wonderful Heavenly Daddy. I could feel His pain, and it brought me pain. However, He then started to share something that filled Him with joy. He said these words:

"I do have My intimate ones who I cherish in a very special way. When I see worship with banners and dancing and shouting, I am so filled with joy. These are the ones who know Me as their Daddy Who wants to bless them. These intimate ones are so excited that I am their Daddy. They worship Me in spirit and in truth, and it touches My heart. These children know that My banner over them is My love. These are My children that truly hunger for all that I am. It brings Me such happiness to see My children celebrating and worshiping together, especially when they celebrate My Son. Jesus is reason to celebrate and throw a great big worship party! I love to celebrate Him with you!

"Child, when you celebrate and have a big worship party, we celebrate with you in Heaven. I am longing for the day that we will all be together celebrating forever. Beloved, thank you for getting to know Me intimately. When you do, it touches My heart deeply."

Song of Solomon 2:4; Colossians 1:13; Romans 8:16-17; John 4:24

Prayer: Heavenly Daddy, thank You for Your incredible banner of love over me. I long to go into the secret place and celebrate Jesus with You. I will dance and sing and let You know how excited I am that I belong to You and Your Kingdom! I want to show You that I am one of Your intimate ones who worships You in spirit and truth. I want to worship until I feel Your glory come and saturate me. In Jesus' precious name, Amen.

*Spend some time in worship. Spend some time singing and dancing for your King. If you have any banners, wave them around and lift up Jesus. Show Him that you are one of His intimates and touch His heart and feel His glory come and saturate you.

Spend some time writing to your Heavenly Father explaining to Him why you are excited that He is your Daddy.

_____
_____
_____
_____
_____
_____
_____
_____
_____
_____
_____
_____
_____
_____
_____
_____
_____
_____

~Day 43~

THE KINGDOM IS WITHIN YOU!

"Precious child, the Kingdom of Heaven is within you right now. I tell you that, whether you feel it or not, the Kingdom of Heaven is within you waiting to break out on earth. There is no sickness in My Kingdom. There is no mental illness or discouragement in My Kingdom. Do you need healing? Receive your inheritance now. When you accepted Me, you became a joint heir with Christ. You inherited the Kingdom. You inherited Me! Receive your inheritance.

"Beloved, I am within you! What do you need? Do you need hope? Draw from Me. Do you need healing? Draw from Me. Do you need peace? Draw from Me. Beloved, I am not like a well that dries up. You can continue to draw from Me forever. I love it when you draw what you need from Me. All that I am is yours! Let Me give you this life-changing revelation.

"Precious one, if you feel lifeless and without hope, it is because you do not yet understand what is already yours. It is because you do not yet understand that the Kingdom of Heaven is within you. Do not let the kingdom of darkness deceive you into believing you are lifeless and powerless. That is a lie. The only power the enemy has is the power that you give to him. Because I live in you, you have all the power you need to live the abundant life and fulfill the unique destiny I have for you. I want you to receive this revelation. Believe Me when I tell you that you are full of health, life, power, and love because the Kingdom is within you. In fact, the same power that raised Christ from the dead lives in you!"

Luke 17:21; Galatians 3:26-29; Romans 8:16-17; Ephesians 1:19-20; Colossians 1:27

Prayer:

Heavenly Daddy, thank You that Christ lives in me, the hope of glory. Thank You for reminding me that because Christ is in me, the Kingdom of Heaven is within me. Help me to receive this truth in my heart. In Jesus' precious name, Amen.

*Proclaim throughout the day, "The same power that raised Christ from the dead lives in me!" Thank Jesus that He lives in you and that you can draw anything you need from Him. Lift up His holy name.

Write down all the things that are inside you because Jesus lives in you.

~Day 44~

YOU ARE UNIQUE

"My beloved, do you see how I created different trees for you to enjoy and all sorts of flowers with unique blooms? Did you notice how many different animal species I created? It is no different with My children. I created each of you with a unique purpose. You are unique.

"Do not let the enemy get you into comparing yourself and your calling to others. Beloved, do not let anyone tell you that you need to be more like they are. You are unique. Don't try to become someone you are not because it will only bring you more frustration. I want you to be free in who I created you to be. I want you to love yourself. I want you to love who I created you to be. I want you to be transformed into My image, not someone else's.

"Child, it grieves Me when you listen to the lies of the enemy that tell you that you should be different. It grieves Me when you 'beat yourself up' with his lies. I tell you to renew your mind with the truth that you are unique and I love your uniqueness. I love you just the way you are, and I always will.

Child, if you dislike yourself because of sin in your life, let Me help you with it. Let Me show you how to overcome. I see your heart, and I see how you don't want to sin, but how you are struggling to overcome in your own strength. Child, let Me live through you. Let My Spirit cause you to rise up. The victory is yours, and don't let the enemy deceive you into thinking that you will never stop failing in a certain area. No, I tell you that you are an overcomer because of what I purchased for you on the cross. Child, that sin that you hate is not part of you. It is not who you are. Remember that. Having hatred for sin in your life is good, but don't let the enemy deceive you into thinking that you don't deserve to love yourself or you don't deserve My love because of any sin struggles. That is a lie. I took your sins as far as the East is from the West. I now focus on you and how much I love and adore you. I focus on your uniqueness. I love that all of My children are unique. Be free to enjoy your uniqueness the way I do."

Psalm 139; 2 Corinthians 3:18; Psalm 103

Prayer:

Heavenly Daddy, thank You for reminding me that I don't have to try to be someone else. I'm sorry for the times that I don't love myself. Daddy, help me to truly see myself the way You see me so that I can love who I was created to be. In Jesus' name, Amen.

*Thank your Heavenly Daddy for your uniqueness and embrace who you were created to be.

Spend some time writing down ways in which you are unique.

~Day 45~

FEAR NOT!

"My precious child, a huge weapon the enemy uses against you is fear. I tell you, fear not, for I am with you. Let Me remind you again that I am for you, not against you. I have plans to prosper you and not to harm you. I am for you, not against you. Fear is the opposite of who you are because you are a new creation in Me. I am peace. I am love. I am joy.

"The enemy comes and tells you many lies about why you should fear. These are all lies from the eternal pit of hell. The truth is that the kingdom of darkness is filled with fear. They have reason to fear. They know their time is short. They know they are already defeated. They know they will spend eternity without Me, which fills them with fear and terror. Child, fear not! I have translated you out of the kingdom of darkness into My Kingdom. My Kingdom is filled with peace, not fear! Remind yourself that you live in this world, but you are from a different world. You belong to My Kingdom, and peace, not fear, is your inheritance.

"Beloved, take a stand against the lying kingdom that tells you to stay in fear. Believe the truth and the truth will set you free. The truth is that I have not given you a spirit of fear, but I have given you power, love, and a sound mind. Take a stand against fear in My name. I crushed fear on the cross! Fear not. Let my perfect love take it all from you now. You are My precious child, and I love you more than you could ever imagine, and I am always with you."

Isaiah 41:10; 1 John 4:8; Colossians 1:13; John 15:19; 2 Timothy 1:7

Prayer:

Heavenly Father, I thank You for reminding me that fear does not come from You. Father, I pray that You would help me to trust You in all things. Help me to trust that You are my Daddy that takes care of me. Thank You for reminding me that You are protecting me and You have plans to prosper me and not harm me. Show me the lies of the enemy that I have been believing and help me to replace them with the truth that I have nothing to fear because You are always with me. Help me to know Your perfect love that casts out all fear in a special way today. In Jesus' name, Amen.

*Start paying attention to any thoughts of fear that come in throughout the day and get rid of them as soon as they come to your mind. Remind yourself that fear is not from Daddy. Renew your mind that you have nothing to fear because He is on your side. Renew your mind with Scriptures that stand against fear.

Write down several times, "Fear is the opposite of who I am because I am a New Creation in Jesus. If My Daddy is for me, who can be against me?" Write a letter to your Daddy telling Him why you can trust Him.

~Day 46~

LET ME BREAK DOWN THE WALLS

I saw a very touching picture of Jesus. First, I saw a woman who was crying. She was saying, "Jesus, I want to experience your love for me, but I can't feel it. I want to know it. I know there is so much more, but there is something preventing me from receiving it." As the woman continued to weep, I saw that in front of the woman, there was a huge wall. On the other side of the wall, I saw Jesus. He was filled with so much compassion and love for this woman. I saw Him take an ax and He started beating the ax against the wall. He was breaking the wall down little by little while He was filled with so much love and compassion for the woman. Then, I heard these words:

"Beloved, sometimes you have walls up that prevent you from receiving all of the love I have for you. I see you frustrated in not being able to receive. I am filled with so much love and compassion for you during these painful times. I will never stop pursuing you with My unending, passionate love. Let Me show you why you have walls up. I know that it is pain and hurt that cause you to erect and keep a wall up that blocks you from receiving. Let Me heal that pain for you. Give it to Me. Ask Me to show you what it is and listen for My voice. I want it to go, and so do you.

"Beloved, sometimes there is a wall of un-forgiveness that prevents you from fully experiencing my love for you and the love of others. Precious one, it is time to let un-forgiveness go so that you can go higher. Let it go. When you let all un-forgiveness go, you will reach a higher spiritual level. It will be better than you ever dreamed possible. You will feel free. Let Me help you take down that wall of un-forgiveness. Let Me help you destroy the wall. I long for you to be completely healed.

"Child, I love you more than you could ever imagine. When you are in pain, I am so filled with compassion for you. I see every tear that falls. Your pain and hurt do not go unnoticed by Me. Beloved, let Me help you take down those walls today and give you the desire of your heart."

Luke 17:3-4

Prayer: Jesus, thank You so much for this touching picture because I struggle in this area. I pray that You would show me any walls that I have up that prevent me from fully receiving the love that You have for me, which is actually already inside of me, poured out by the Holy Spirit. Show me if I have any un-forgiveness towards anyone so I can get rid of it. In Jesus' name, Amen.

*Picture Jesus breaking down your walls as He is filled with compassion.

Write down your thoughts about this touching vision.
Pour your heart out to Jesus.

~Day 47~

THE OIL OF JOY FROM JESUS

I saw a vision of Jesus. I saw oil flowing from His nail-pierced hands and feet. It was flowing from Heaven to earth on certain people. I saw that some people had a little bit on them, but those that were drenched in this oil of joy had so much joy and peace. They were full of joy and laughing non-stop. I heard the Lord give me these words:

"My desire is for every single human being on the earth to know what My Son went through for them. When they get a deep revelation of His love and what He endured on their behalf, they will be drenched in the oil of joy that comes from My Son.

"Child, it was in the garden of Gethsemane, which means oil press, that Jesus was full of agony, knowing the cup that He would endure because of His great love for you. During this time, He was rejected and full of agony of soul. He knew that He would be crushed in order to reconcile the world to Me. Precious child, know that in the same way olives are pressed and crushed to produce oil, My Son was brutally crushed for your complete forgiveness, healing, and salvation, and so much more. He was crushed because of His deep, deep love for you.

"Beloved, because of what My Son went through, you now have an inheritance to live an abundant life filled with joy. Receive the oil of joy that comes from getting a deep revelation that Jesus finished it all for you. When He said, 'It is finished,' He meant, 'It is finished. I went through this for you, My beloved. I purchased your victory.' Let Me pour this oil of joy all over you.

"Child, do you want a deeper revelation of Jesus and what He went through on the cross? Do you want a deeper revelation of what the finished work of My Son means for you right now? Ask Me. Let Me really show you. Come into the secret place and let Me show you the cross."

Isaiah 61:3; Luke 22:39-46; Ephesians 1:3-9; John 19:30; 1 Corinthians 2:2; Hebrews 1:9

Prayer:

Heavenly Daddy, I thank You for giving me a deeper revelation of the cross. Thank You for showing me personally what Jesus went through for me. I pray that I would feel this oil of joy flowing from Jesus' hands and feet from the inside out and that it would spread to others. In Jesus' name, Amen.

*Ask Jesus for the oil of joy to be poured out all over you today.

Spend some time writing a letter to Jesus thanking Him for the oil of joy.
Share with Him why you need the oil of joy in your life.

_____

_____

_____

_____

_____

_____

_____

_____

_____

_____

_____

_____

_____

_____

_____

_____

_____

_____

_____

_____

~Day 48~

I AM YOUR LOVER!

"Come away, My love, My darling. I long for your sweet kisses, your warm embrace. I enjoy every part of you. Your touch is like fine wine. Your voice is like honey dripping from the heavens. You are beautiful, My bride. Come away with Me. Abandon everyone and everything and come and truly be with Me in the secret place. You will not be disappointed. Let Me take you away to Myself. Let Me passionately love you like no other has ever loved you. No other can love you like I can. No other can satisfy the desires of your heart like I can.

"One touch of My love and you are lost in the moment. I am a passionate lover. I am faithful to all who love Me. I am faithful to all who desire My love. Come away and you will find your true love. Come away with Me and find the deep, deep love you have been searching and longing for your whole life. I am holding you in my arms right now and giving you sweet love kisses. Do you feel My presence with you right now? Do you sense My presence? Your lover is here with you right now, and I will never leave your side. Come, let Me gaze into your eyes with My eyes of fire. Let Me burn off all doubt that I love you. Come away with Me, my love. Come and let Me show you how much I adore you. Whenever I hear your sweet voice speaking to Me, My heart melts with love for you. You will always be the beautiful bride I have chosen to be Mine forever! I cherish you, My bride."

Song of Solomon; Psalm 37:4; Isaiah 54:5

Prayer:

Jesus, I long to know You as my passionate lover. Show me how passionate Your love is for me. Let me feel it. Show me any barriers that are preventing me from experiencing Your burning, everlasting love for me. I want to remove all obstacles from receiving my inheritance of a passionate love affair with You, Jesus. In the business of the day, whisper in my ear that You want to speak to me in the secret place. I pray that I would be sensitive to hearing Your voice whispering sweet nothings in my ear. I love You, Jesus! Thank You for being my husband forever. In Your precious name, Amen.

*Spend some time telling Jesus that you always want Him to be your first love. Tell Him over and over again today until it is truly the desire of your heart.

*Spend some time writing the most passionate love letter
you have ever written to Jesus. He will treasure this letter in His heart.*

~Day 49~

THE BOOK OF LIFE VISION

I saw a vision of a Christian man walking with his head down in shame. I saw Satan and his demons showing the man a scroll with all of his sins on it. They kept pointing to it, condemning the man as he walked in shame.

Next, I saw the man go read his Bible. However, the enemy came in and showed him the scroll with all of his sins, so the man felt too ashamed to read the Word.

After abandoning the Word, I saw this same man try to put on praise and worship music, but the enemy came in and showed him the scroll again, shouting condemning thoughts to him, and the man abandoned the idea of worship.

Next, I saw this same man walking into church, but the enemy showed him his scroll and the scrolls of others that had a lot fewer sins written on them. The man walked out of church in shame.

Then, suddenly, I saw Jesus appear as the enemy was condemning this man. I saw him show Satan and his demons the nail holes in his hands. I heard Him say, "And I will forgive their wickedness, and I will never again remember their sins" (Hebrews 8:12 NLT). The enemy left. I then heard Jesus say to the man, "Son, where are your condemners?" And the man said, "They left." And Jesus said, "I will never show you this scroll." Jesus then ripped up the scroll of sins, and then He took out the Book of Life. He opened the Book of Life and showed the man his name in the book. He said, "I have come to give life not to condemn. I was condemned at the cross for you, My son. Go in peace and live the abundant life that I so freely gave you."

Revelation 12:10; Hebrews 8:12; John 10:10

Prayer:

Thank You Jesus for taking my sin and punishment on the cross. Anytime the enemy comes to condemn me with my failures, I will remind him that You defeated him for me and took all of my sins upon You on the cross so that I could be free. All the glory to Jesus, Amen.

*Spend some time thanking Jesus for giving you life instead of death. Thank Him for taking away all of your guilt and shame. Thank Him for loving you so much that He came to give you an abundant life. Worship Him with your whole heart.

Spend some time reflecting on how the enemy tries to attack you with guilt and condemnation over sin. How will you handle it the next time he tries to steal your peace? Spend some time journaling about what the "abundant life" means to you and thank Jesus for purchasing it for you.

~Day 50~

COME TO ME FOR ALL COMFORT AND I WILL COMFORT YOU

"Beloved, come to Me when you feel sad or wounded. Let Me comfort you with My loving words and embrace. Sometimes you are tempted to go to other things. Beloved, if you come to Me, you will experience My comfort and love in a deeper way. Let Me comfort you the way you have never been comforted before.

"Come into the secret place and wait on Me, and I will give you the comfort and strength you need to rise above your trials. Let Me show you that I can comfort you like no other. Child, I know that when you are feeling emotional pain, it hurts. It hurts a lot! I know it makes you want to escape or even sometimes come and be with Me in Heaven. Sometimes the enemy even tells you that things will never get better until you leave this earth and get to glory. That is a lie! I want you to experience the abundant life that I came to give you.

"Beloved, I know that you have gone to other things for comfort your whole life, but I challenge you to give Me a chance. Let Me comfort you. Come and weep in My arms and let Me encourage you. Those other things you go to do not encourage you. They prolong the pain and make it worse. They don't work because you were created to come to Me for all comfort. Let Me show you that you are more than a conqueror. Let Me show you that My Spirit can breathe life back into you. Let Me show you how I can turn pain into a powerful testimony to help others.

"Come to Me when you need comfort. I WILL comfort you. I WILL love on you. I WILL kiss you and breathe life back into you. When you come to Me for comfort, you will experience the victory and breakthrough you have been waiting for. Come, I am waiting precious child of Mine."

John 14:26; Romans 8:37; Isaiah 40:31

Prayer:

Heavenly Daddy, when I am in pain, I am so used to going to other sources for comfort. I want to change that today. Help me to come to You when I am in pain. Help me to feel Your loving arms wrapped around me. Remind me that You promise to comfort me. Thank You so much for taking care of me Daddy. In Jesus' name, Amen.

*If you need comfort, run into Daddy's arms right now and receive His love and comfort for you.

*Spend some time writing a letter to Daddy telling Him why
you want to come to Him for all comfort instead of going to other things.
See what comes up and share your heart.*

_____
_____
_____
_____
_____
_____
_____
_____
_____
_____
_____
_____
_____
_____
_____
_____
_____
_____

~Day 51~

YOU HAVE A DESTINY!

"Beloved, you have a destiny. You have a special calling in My Kingdom. All of My children have a destiny whether they realize it or not. Sometimes the enemy comes to try to steal, kill, and destroy the destiny I have for you. That kingdom of darkness comes in with discouragement and tells you that you are not important in My Kingdom. He even uses human vessels to discourage you. I tell you those are lies from the pit of hell. I do have a mighty destiny just for you.

"Precious one, the enemy also likes to come in and make you compare yourself to others. That is a weapon of the enemy to keep you discouraged and in self-pity and to keep you from fulfilling the call I have on your life. Say no to any discouragement. I want you to look in the mirror and proclaim and decree, 'My Heavenly Daddy has a mighty destiny and calling on my life and I will fulfill it with His help and in His timing!' Keep believing and proclaiming!

"Beloved, sometimes My timing is not your timing. I promise things will happen when you are ready. Sometimes I need to do healing in My children before they are ready to step out into their destiny. If they go before their time, they are more susceptible to the enemy's lies, temptations, and destruction. I don't want this to happen to you. I want you to be ready and filled with My love and My power and My truth.

"Come into the secret place and let Me confirm to you that you have a mighty destiny. It brings Me great joy that you belong to My Kingdom, My royal child."

John 10:10; Jeremiah 29:11; 1 Peter 2:9

Prayer:

Heavenly Father, I vow to take a stand against all discouragement that comes in different forms from the enemy to try to steal the mighty calling You have on my life. I will start proclaiming that I have a mighty destiny and You are preparing me for it even now. Thank You for encouraging me, Daddy God. In Jesus' name, Amen.

*Start thanking your Heavenly Daddy for your destiny. Cancel any assignments of the enemy over that destiny and start decreeing and proclaiming victory. Thank Him for the unique destiny that He has for you.

Write a letter to Daddy telling Him what your heart's desire is regarding your destiny. Let Him speak to you as you write and pray. Write out several times: "I will not let the enemy steal my destiny. I will not go into discouragement. I trust My Daddy has good plans for me."

_____
_____
_____
_____
_____
_____
_____
_____
_____
_____
_____
_____
_____
_____
_____
_____
_____
_____
_____
_____

~Day 52~

I WANT YOU TO TRUST MY LOVE!

"My sweet darling, My love is the most pure love you could ever receive. My love is the most healing love you will ever know. My love brings so much peace and joy, and I want you to experience this in a deep, deep way in your life. Will you receive My love for you? It brings Me great joy when My precious children receive all that I have for them. Beloved, just say, 'Yes, I receive Your love, Heavenly Daddy.' and you will feel Me pour My liquid love from Heaven all over you. Just receive! You cannot love yourself and others until you receive My love for you.

"Beloved, you can trust My love. You can trust that I will never hurt you. I know that people may have wounded you and hurt you, but I tell you that I will never hurt you! I am not like people, My love is pure. My love is holy. My love is not painful. My love will never hurt you. You can trust My love. When you receive My love, you receive Me because I am love!

"Beloved, I want to take down all of the walls in your life that have prevented you from fully experiencing My love that is already poured inside you by Holy Spirit. Will you let Me? Let Me heal all of your wounds that cause you to think that you can't trust My love or anyone else's. I will not hurt you. Let My love crush those walls and those wounds from people who have hurt you. My love is the solution to all of the pain in your life. When you receive My love, it will help you to trust others and not feel so wounded and rejected when they fail you. You will see that they, too, have wounds, and people who are hurting hurt others around them until they fully know and receive My healing love. Pray for those that hurt you to receive My love. You will be blessed when you pray for them. You will start to see them through My eyes, and you will be healed in more ways than you can imagine."

1 John 4:16, 19; Jeremiah 29:11; 31:3; Romans 5:5; Matthew 5:44

Prayer:

Heavenly Daddy, thank You so much for the healing, eternal love You have for me. Help me to receive it today in a special way. Thank You that Your love never fails even when I do. Your love is precious to me, and I receive it. In Jesus' name, Amen!

*Remind yourself throughout the day, "I can trust my Daddy's love."

Spend some time writing your Heavenly Daddy a letter telling Him that you want to feel His liquid love from Heaven all over you. Tell Him you want the love that is already poured inside you by Holy Spirit to break out in your life. Tell Him why you can trust His pure, holy love.

~Day 53~

LET ME WRITE YOU A LOVE LETTER

"Beloved child of Mine, get a pen. Come into My presence. I want to give you a fresh love letter from My heart. My Word is a love letter to you, but today, I want to give you a fresh love letter for you to carry around with you to remind you of how much I adore you. This is a "now" word for you.

"Get your pen and paper and go to the secret place. You will be truly blessed. My Words are life. My Words are spiritual food to your body. My Words break all discouragement. My Words break all condemnation, guilt, and shame. My Words will bring healing to your body and soul. Do you need healing? Come to Me now and let Me heal you.

"Come, I want to speak to you. I am your Heavenly Daddy, and I want to share with you how much I love you. Come and listen! Start writing My love-filled words that are just for you. Let these truths set you free to be yourself with Me. I love you just the way you are, My precious child."

John 6:63; 15:7; 8:32

Prayer:

Heavenly Daddy, I come to You right now with my pen and paper, and I ask You in faith to speak to me and let me write down Your words of love to me. I tell the enemy that he cannot interfere with Holy Spirit's voice in the name of Jesus. Holy Spirit, please tell me what I need to hear today. Thank You for loving me so much that You want to speak to me and love on me. Help these words to penetrate my spirit and transform my life. In Jesus' name, Amen.

*Spend some time listening to Holy Spirit. Ask Him for a love letter to you and/or any Scriptures that He wants to speak over you. Write down what He is saying to you personally.

*After receiving Daddy's love letter to you, write one to Him. Pour your heart out in it, and let Him know how much you love Him. Put it in an envelope and address it to Him and then, in faith, offer it up to Him. Then, put it in a safe place and read it in the future. You will be so blessed, and Daddy will be touched.

Write Heavenly Daddy a love letter and bless Him with your love.

~Day 54~

BLISS FLOWING FROM THE CROSS

I saw a vision of the soldier pierce Jesus' side when He had given up His Spirit. I saw, in the Spirit, blood and water flowing from His side, and then it proceeded to start gushing. I saw the water and blood flowing like a powerful waterfall, and it was drenching all of God's children. I saw them being drenched and almost overpowered by the force of the blood and water waterfall. Then, I saw all of the people filled with unspeakable joy. They were so filled with joy they could hardly contain themselves. I saw them laughing and dancing. I then saw them start praising Jesus. They couldn't stop praising Jesus, which only increased the ecstasy they were feeling. They were blasted and overwhelmed with the joy of Jesus, the joy of the cross. Then I heard these words:

"My beloved, there is a joy that flows from the cross unto My children. When you get a revelation of My finished work, you will come to know a pleasure you never imagined possible. I want you to know that this bliss, this ecstasy, this delight is your inheritance as My blood-bought child. You were created to feel My joy and love. You were created to feel the bliss of the cross as My New Covenant child.

"Precious one, are you lacking joy? Let Me give you a fresh revelation of what I accomplished on the cross. Let Me give you a revelation that you are a new creation now because of what I did for you. Let Me show you that I took all depression and crucified it on the cross with your old man. You are a new creation in Me. Joy lives in you. Let it break out. Don't hold it back. Let it break out and explode. Let Me help you remove any walls that prevent you from experiencing My bliss. Let Me give you a deeper revelation of who I am so that you can see what is already in you because I live in you. When you see who I am, you can't help but offer up praises, and, when you do, the bliss increases until you are overpowered with joy.

"See yourself covered in My blood. See yourself refreshed by the living water. It all flows from a deep revelation of the cross. Child, I want you to receive the bliss that flows from the cross."

After I heard these words, I saw a vision of Jesus laughing hysterically. He was filled with ecstasy and joy. He said, "This is who I am."

John 19:34; Luke 22:20; Galatians 5:22; 2 Corinthians 5:17; Romans 6:6

*Start praising Jesus and thanking Him for the cross until you feel the bliss flowing from the cross.

Spend some time journaling what this vision means to you personally.

_____
_____
_____
_____
_____
_____
_____
_____
_____
_____
_____
_____
_____
_____
_____
_____
_____
_____
_____
_____
_____
_____
_____
_____

~Day 55~

YOU ARE UNDER GRACE - PART 1

I saw a vision of two mountains. One was Mt. Sinai (where the law was given), and the other was Mt. Zion. On top of the mountains, connecting the two, were the stone tablets of the Ten Commandments. The stone tablets were a barrier between the heavens and the earth. Next, I saw a vision of Jesus enduring the cross. With every lash and beating, I would see the stone tablets of the Ten Commandments start to crumble. With each lash, they continued to crumble. With each nail, I saw the stone tablets disintegrate into little stones. When Jesus gave up His Spirit, I saw the veil being torn in two, then I saw the rest of the stone tablets fall to the ground. It became a big pile of stones. I heard Him say these words:

"You are under a New Covenant of grace. The old is obsolete. Your acceptance is no longer based on whether you live up to the law. I worked and toiled that day so that you would no longer have to work to be forgiven or receive the blessings. I did it all for you. I took the law and nailed it to the cross to show you that there is a new way of the Spirit. Do not look to the law to make you accepted, you are under grace. This is freedom. I set you free from the penalty of the law. I set you free from the curse of the law. I set you free. Do you know why? It is because I wanted you to live a free, abundant life. I set you free. When you know I set you free because of My love for you, you do not have to strive to live a holy life. This is freedom. Let the Spirit rule your life. Where the Spirit of the Lord is, there is freedom and rest!

"I am the one that gave you right standing. The law's goal is to point you to Me, your freedom. It shows you how much you need Me in your life. Because of My shed blood, you are now free to come boldly into My presence at any time because your faith in Me has made you forever righteous in My sight. Let this good news help you fall deeper in love with your Savior."

Ephesians 1:15; Colossians 2:14; Hebrews 8:13; 12:22; Acts 13:39; Galatians 3:10-11; 5:4, 16, 19, 21, 24-25; 4:5, 12; 5:1, 4, 14; Romans 6:14; Jeremiah 31:33; 2 Corinthians 5:17; 3:17; Hebrews 12:22

Prayer:

Thank You Jesus for making me a New Covenant child under grace. Thank You that I can now come boldly to the throne of grace because Your precious blood has set me free. Thank You that Your Spirit in me sets me free and helps me to live a holy life that I could never do on my own. In Your name, Amen

Write a letter to Daddy telling Him how much it means to you to be a New Covenant child of His.

_____

_____

_____

_____

_____

_____

_____

_____

_____

_____

_____

_____

_____

_____

_____

_____

_____

_____

_____

_____

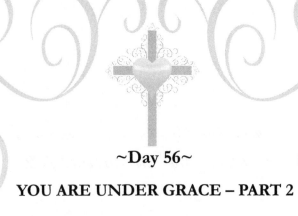

~Day 56~

YOU ARE UNDER GRACE – PART 2

Jesus again showed me the pile of stones from the previous vision where the stone tablets crumbled when He endured the cross. The pile was so enormous that it was the size of several mountains. I asked Jesus what the stones represented. He said, "This pile of stones represents all of the stonings that could have taken place had I not died on the cross. I took your punishment. I took the punishment for every single law broken. Only I was capable of obeying the entire law for the entire world. Under grace and the New Covenant, I took the punishment and wrath for the entire world for all of their sins."

Next, I saw a very touching picture. I saw this pile of stones being crushed and made into cement. Jesus took the cement and molded it into individual cement hearts for the entire world. He said, "Just as those rocks were crushed and made into cement, I was crushed for the entire world. I was willingly crushed all because of My passionate love for them. I was crushed so that they could become a new creation, living a life by the Spirit. I was crushed so that My people could be filled with Me and so that I could help them to live a life by the Spirit, a holy life, no longer slaves to the law." I saw Jesus taking the plaques and personally derlivering them to everyone in the world. He said this:

"I want everyone to know how much I personally love and care for them. I want them to know what I went through so that they realize the love I have for them.

"Child who is reading this, I love you so much. You are so precious and dear to Me. Imagine Me being crushed for your sins, taking your punishment, and making you righteous. That is what is represented by stones being crushed to become hearts. It brought Me joy to take your punishment. This is love. I took it all because you are so incredibly precious to Me. Receive this in your heart. I love you. I love you. I love you. Feel My arms wrapped around you right now."

Isaiah 53:5; Colossians 1:27; Galatians 5:1; 2 Corinthians 5:21; Romans 8; Romans 6:23

Prayer:

Thank You Jesus for being crushed for my freedom. You are so precious to me. Let me experience You in a new way today in the secret place. In Your precious name, Amen.

*Spend some time praising Jesus for His amazing love. Thank Him for setting you free. Thank Him for being crushed for you to set you free from the law of sin and death.

Look up Luke 22:44. Spend some time writing Jesus a letter from your heart thanking Him for taking your cup of wrath.

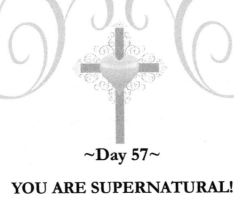

~Day 57~

YOU ARE SUPERNATURAL!

"My precious child, I love it when you hunger for the invisible realm more than the visible. The invisible realm is more real than the visible. If you only knew what I have prepared for you for all eternity, it would overwhelm you. I cannot wait for you to see what awaits you, My beloved. I know the things that you love, and I have prepared something specifically for you to enjoy forever. What I have prepared for you will never be destroyed or ruined. It is more real than the visible world you see around you.

"Beloved, I see you hungering to see the invisible realm. I see how you cry out to Me to open your eyes to see into the spiritual realm. Precious one, I hear your cries. I hear every single one of them, and I tell you to keep seeking Me and I will give you the desires of your heart. I see you crying out to Me to see angels, to see the sick recover, to see demons flee from people, and even to see the dead raised to life. I see your hunger for open-eyed visions, dreams, and words of knowledge. It is not wrong to hunger for these things when you are seeking Me.

"I am supernatural! When you hunger for supernatural things, you hunger for more of who I am. You are a supernatural being and everything supernatural is your inheritance. The supernatural lives in you! The glory lives in you! Supernatural power lives in you. Keep asking Me for this revelation, and you will receive it. Start proclaiming that you are supernatural. Start proclaiming that the same power that raised Christ from the dead lives in you! Keep proclaiming this until the revelation reaches your spirit.

"Child, battle any lies of the evil one that tell you that you are not worthy to receive your supernatural inheritance. Ignore lies that say you are not receiving because I think of you as inferior. These are lies from the pit of hell to keep you discouraged. When you are discouraged, you lose the faith to receive this revelation. This is a huge tactic of the enemy. Child, don't get discouraged. Keep seeking what is rightfully yours. Ask Me to give you a revelation that you are supernatural because Christ is in you, the hope of glory!"

Colossians 1:16, 27; Joel 2:28; Mark 16:17-18; Romans 8:11

Prayer:

Heavenly Daddy, help me to hunger for more of You and who You are. Daddy, I will not fall into discouragement, a scheme of the enemy. Rather, I will remain in faith that this is my inheritance. In Jesus' name, Amen.

Pour out your heart to your Daddy about how you want your supernatural inheritance. What is your heart's desire? Don't hold back. Pour out your heart to Him and let Him speak to you. If you desire, break off all discouragement and pray that Daddy will activate your spiritual senses.

~Day 58~

WHOSE REPORT WILL YOU BELIEVE?

I saw a vision. It had two parts to it. In the first vision, I saw people looking up to Heaven every time they did something wrong, and they thought they saw Jesus with a frown on His face making a long list of their sins. These people saw this and went running, looking down in shame. In the second part of the vision, I saw these same people looking up to Heaven when they sinned, and they saw Jesus with arms wide open asking them to come into His embrace. As I looked at Him, His arms out for a hug became a picture of His arms nailed to the cross. He had the most loving smile on His face. These same people felt loved, accepted Jesus' forgiveness, and went away feeling peace. Next, I heard these words:

"Beloved, whose report will you believe? The first vision is the enemy's report. He lies to you about who I am and how I feel about you. He tells you that I am counting your sins against you and that I can't wait to punish you for them. He tells you that I am constantly disappointed and am always wondering, "When is she going to get it right?' Beloved, this is one of the greatest tactics of the enemy to keep My children in bondage. They run from Me, and My love becomes very, very distant. They start to fear Me and even dislike Me. I understand why they behave like this when they believe the lies from the enemy. I understand why they would want to run and hide. However, it grieves Me because it is not the truth.

"The second vision is the true report. My Son was the final sacrifice for sins. I love you so much. I want you to come boldly to My throne of grace. I want you to see how I see you. Whose report will you believe? When you believe My report, you are able to feel My love. My love becomes real and not distant. I become real in your life. Our relationship deepens because you start trusting Me more and more when you believe that I love you and am not constantly looking for reasons to condemn you. Jesus took all your condemnation, My beloved. When I look at you, I look at all the reasons why I love and adore you so much. I say, "Wow, this child is so precious and unique to Me. I am so glad she is created in My image and she belongs to Me. Receive this truth for your heart."

Psalm 103:3; Hebrews 10; 4:16; 2 Corinthians 5:21; Romans 8:1

Prayer:

Heavenly Daddy, thank You so much for reminding me that You are not up there constantly condemning me, rather, You have sent Holy Spirit to remind me how much You love me, and He reminds me of the righteousness that Jesus purchased for me. This is amazing news. It makes me fall deeper in love with You. It brings me peace. In Jesus' name, Amen.

Spend some time reflecting on Hebrews 4:16.
Journal about what it means to come "boldly" into Daddy's presence.

_____

_____

_____

_____

_____

_____

_____

_____

_____

_____

_____

_____

_____

_____

_____

_____

_____

_____

_____

_____

_____

~Day 59~

I CAME TO GET YOU!

"My child, there is nothing I wouldn't do for you. My love burns for you. There are no earthly words to adequately describe how I feel about you. I have whispered, "I love you" in your ear more than the number of grains of sand on the entire earth! If each drop of water in the oceans represented each time I said, "I adore you," not even all the water on the entire earth would be enough. I want you to know how much I love and adore you. There is nothing I wouldn't do for you, My precious one!

"My greatest love act for you was on the cross and all that My finished work represents for you. I laid My life down for you and became darkness all because of My extreme love for you. I came down from Heaven, emptied Myself of everything, and laid down my life for you so that I could bring you into a new life with Me forever. I came to get you. I came to save you and set you free. You were on My mind while I was being tortured. I was in excruciating emotional and physical pain, but it was all worth it knowing that I came to get you to bring you into My Kingdom to be seated in Heavenly places with Me. The emotional pain I went through from being separated from My Father was brutal. It was torturous. Yet, it was worth it to receive you as My precious treasure forever. Yes, I call you My treasure. You were the treasure I came to get when I emptied Myself. You are My precious treasure that I value beyond words. My treasure chest in Heaven would not be complete without you in it.

"Beloved, never forget that you are Mine and I am taking care of you. Never forget that I came to get you so that we could spend eternity together in each other's arms."

John 15:13; Philippians 2:5-8; John 3:17; Isaiah 53:5; Matthew 27:45-46; Ephesians 2:6-7

Prayer:

Heavenly Daddy, help me to understand that I am seated with You in Heavenly places right now. Help me to understand that Jesus came to get me to bring me into Your Kingdom. Show me in a special way today that I am Your treasure. Thank You for saving me and setting me free. In Jesus' name, Amen.

*Today, keep reminding yourself, "I am My Heavenly Daddy's treasure forever."

Write a letter to Jesus telling Him how it makes you feel knowing that He emptied Himself to come to get you. Love on Him.

~Day 60~

I LOVE TO CHEER YOU ON!

I saw a vision of Jesus with a woman. The woman was running a race. Jesus was in front of the woman looking into her eyes and cheering her on. He was running with her. He was saying, "You can do it, you can do it!" Whenever the woman took her eyes off Jesus, she got tired and stopped. However, Jesus would encourage her to continue and to keep her eyes fixed on Him. As soon as the woman looked into His eyes, she was able to get back up and continue running the race as Jesus continually cheered for her. I heard these words:

"My precious child, I love to cheer you on. I am your biggest cheerleader! I love to see you succeed. I love to watch you run the race. Keep your eyes focused and fixed on Me, and I will give you the strength to keep running, to keep moving forward. Keep your eyes fixed on Me. The enemy will try to distract you with many things during this race. He will throw obstacles in your way. However, when you keep your eyes fixed on Me, I guide you and move you around the obstacles. I show you the way to go. I protect you from the schemes and tactics of the enemy.

"Precious one, I ran a race. I got the prize. I ran a race to the cross. I kept My eyes focused on My Father. He continually gave Me the strength to endure what I needed to endure. He helped Me to win the prize. The prize that I won is so valuable to Me; it is worth more than the greatest treasures in Heaven. That prize is you! You were the joy set before Me. You were the one worth going through the pain for. You are My prize. You are worth it all."

Hebrews 12:1-2

Prayer:

Jesus, thank You so much for being my biggest cheerleader. Whenever I take my eyes off of You, prompt me to get rid of any distractions and put my focus back on You. You are so incredibly precious to me. In Your name, Amen.

*Spend some time thanking Jesus for how He is continually cheering for you. Think of a victory in your life and thank Him for helping you to get that victory.

Journal about what this vision personally means to you.

~Day 61~

COME AWAY WITH ME, MY DARLING!

"My darling, come away with Me. Let Me carry you away from the cares of the world to be with Me. I long to be alone with My precious bride. When we are alone, it's as if no one else is in the room. When we are alone, it's as if you are the only person in the world to Me. You are all that matters to Me in that moment. I do not get distracted when I am with you. I listen to every word you say and it gives Me great pleasure to hear your voice when you are fellowshipping with Me.

"Come, let's go be alone. I want you to share your heart and your secrets with Me. Come, let Me share My intimate secrets with you, My favorite one. I long to spend time alone with you, My beautiful, radiant bride.

"Come, be alone with Me and others will see your radiant face as you experience My glory. Come be alone with Me and let Me transform you with My love. I deeply desire intimate relationship with you. I'm waiting with open arms. Come, My darling. Come be with your bridegroom. Come, My love, let's go into the secret place. You are so precious to Me."

Psalm 91:1; Ephesians 3:18; Isaiah 54:5

Prayer:

Jesus, help me to set aside time to be alone with You. I long to share my heart and my deep secrets with You. Give me a holy hunger that cannot be satisfied unless I am in Your presence. Jesus, please give me a deep desire to hear Your sweet voice talking to me and loving on me. Jesus, I want to be one of the intimate ones You share Your secrets with. You are the only one that can satisfy the longings and desires of my heart. I want to see Your glory today. I want my face to radiate Your light to witness Your love to others around me. Thank You so much for desiring to spend time with me. I love You. In Your name, Amen.

*Spend some time alone loving on your lover. He is worth it. Thank Him for being your faithful husband.

Write down something you have never told Jesus before.

~Day 62~

YOU HAVE TOUCHED MY HEART!

"What is that sound? I hear it. It's the sound of My lover. I hear the sound of My bride's voice. I hear her sweet voice praising Me. I hear My lover worshiping Me, and it brings Me such joy. I know that when she worships and praises Me, her heart is filled with such peace, and she experiences My love for her.

"What's that sound? It's My lover. She is weeping, weeping because she is starting to experience how I truly see her. She is weeping as she feels My loving arms wrapped around her. I love that sound. It is precious to Me. It touches My heart deeply when My bride receives a revelation of My love."

After hearing those words, I then saw a picture of Jesus. He was facing the woman who had tears in her eyes. He took His hair and gently wiped away her tears and embraced her. Then, He started weeping and saying, "I love you so much, My bride. I love you so much, My beautiful bride. I love you so much. You have touched My heart with your praises, worship, and loving words. You will forever be in My embrace. I love you with an everlasting love."

Jeremiah 31:3

Prayer:

Dear Jesus, thank You so much for making me Your bride. Thank You for reminding me how touched You are when You hear the sound of my voice worshipping You and praising You. I am so overjoyed to hear this and it makes me want to praise and worship You even more! Jesus, let me feel You embrace me and tell me how much You love me, just like in the vision above. Those words are for me, and that vision is of me with You as well. Personalize all of this for me. In Jesus' name, Amen.

*Spend some time praising and lifting up the name of Jesus. Tell Him how He has touched your heart.

Spend some time writing to Jesus telling Him how much joy it brings you to know that you touch His heart when you worship Him and experience His love for you.

~Day 63~

WHOSE MIRROR ARE YOU LOOKING INTO?

"Beloved, whose mirror are you looking into? Are you looking into the enemy's mirror? The enemy's mirror tells you all the things that are wrong with you. When you look into the enemy's mirror and listen to all the negative things he says about you and receive them, you are actually being transformed into his image more than Mine. When you receive his rejection, shame, guilt, unworthiness, and negative thoughts, he wins, and you forget about who you are in Me. His mirror brings depression and hopelessness.

"Child, I want you to look in My mirror. I want you to see My glory. I want you to take a good look at it and receive it and be transformed by it. The more you look into My mirror, the more you will see your true identity as My beloved child. The more you look into My mirror, the more joy and peace you will feel. The more you look into My mirror, the more victory you will have over your trials because you will see Who lives in you and Who gives you the strength over all trials. The more you look into My mirror, the more you will know the truth that will set you completely free.

"The enemy's mirror lies. It is like a mirror that you see at a carnival. When you look into a carnival mirror, your image is distorted. When you look into it, you see a reality that is altered, changed, and misrepresented. It lies. However, I do not lie! I cannot lie! My mirror represents the truth. Let Me show you who you really are. Let Me show you how I see you. In fact, when you look into the mirror, say, 'I am being transformed by the glory of the Lord because I am looking into His mirror!' You will begin to get a revelation of how much I love you, and you will truly be transformed into My image."

2 Corinthians 3:18

Prayer:

Heavenly Father, I repent for believing the lies the enemy has told me when I have looked into his mirror. Father, today I choose to look into Your mirror and not take my eyes off of it. I ask that You help me to truly see my identity in Christ, and I ask to be transformed and changed and that the heavens will be opened over my life. In Jesus' name, Amen.

*Look into a mirror today and tell yourself, "I am beautiful. My Heavenly Daddy adores me. He sees me without a single fault before Him because of Jesus. I am being transformed into His image more and more each day."

Write down some truths that you can say in front of a mirror today.
For example, "I am the righteousness of God in Jesus Christ.
I am My Daddy's beloved."
Then, go and say them several times today in front of a mirror.

~Day 64~

I WEEP WITH YOU

I heard the sound of a waterfall. I could hear the water gushing down to the bottom of the falls. I asked the Lord, "What is that sound?" I heard the Lord say this:

"I have so much love and compassion for My children. When they weep and are hurting, I weep with them. When they cry out to Me in pain, My heart aches for them. The water you hear gushing represents the many tears I have shed for My children. I am compassionate. Many of My children do not understand how much I love them. Many of My children don't truly know Who I am. This saddens Me and causes Me to grieve and weep. My children, I tell you that I love you so much. You are the apple of My eye. I have your names engraved in the palm of My hand. I know every intimate detail about you. I long for you to understand and grasp the deep, deep love I have for you.

"My children, do not hide from Me when you are in pain. Come to Me, and I will wipe away your tears after we weep together for a season. Child, let Me show you how much I love and care for you. Let Me show you that I am your Daddy and I will take care of your EVERY need. Nothing is too small for Me to care about. Nothing is too big for Me to handle. Come to Daddy! Come to Daddy! Come, I am longing to see you run into My arms. Come! Let Me fill you with a Heavenly love you do not know. Come! I will always love you with a supernatural love!"

John 11:35; Romans 12:15; Psalm 17:8; Isaiah 49:16; Isaiah 25:8; Jeremiah 31:3

Prayer:

Heavenly Daddy, help me to understand in a deeper way how much You care for me. Show me that You even weep with me when I am in pain. Help me to come to You with every sorrow and every pain. Remind me that You want to take care of me and help me and guide me through all situations. Help me to see You as My Daddy that loves me and cares so deeply for me that You want to take care of my every need. I choose to come to You right now and ask You to fill me with Your love. Thank You for being My Daddy. In Jesus' name, Amen.

*Picture your Heavenly Daddy weeping with you during times of pain and then see Him wiping your tears away.

Spend some time thanking your Heavenly Daddy for all the times He has shed tears for you and shared in your pain. Thank Him for His comfort during those times.

_____

_____

_____

_____

_____

_____

_____

_____

_____

_____

_____

_____

_____

_____

_____

_____

_____

_____

_____

_____

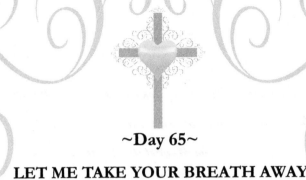

~Day 65~

LET ME TAKE YOUR BREATH AWAY

I saw a painfully touching vision of Jesus. I saw Him with the cross on His back having difficulty breathing with every step He took. Next, I saw Him on the cross after His crucifixion, and He was in pain. He was gasping for air, finding it very difficult to breathe in the position He was in on the cross. He was gasping and struggling to breathe. Finally, He could gasp no more, and He gave up His Spirit. I heard Him say these words:

"My precious child, My passionate love for you took My breath away. My extreme love for you was the reason I endured the cross and gave up My Spirit. My burning love for you took My breath away so that I could take your breath away with My love for all eternity. You are destined to receive this love forever. You are destined to have a passionate love affair with Me, your husband. Child, come into the secret place and let Me take your breath away. You will never be the same.

"Beloved, let Me love you. Let Me be your first love. Let Me be the one to take your breath away. I want you to melt in My arms. I want you to feel Me passionately romancing you and pursuing you with My love. My love does not fade one bit. It never changes. It does not grow cold. It stays ignited for all eternity.

"My lover, I want you to come so close that you can feel My breath as I whisper in your ear how much I love you. I am longing for your presence. I am longing to take your breath away right now. Come, let Me love on you. I tell you that when you speak to Me, you also take My breath away. Come away, My beautiful favored one. I am waiting. I have many love gifts and surprises to give to you. Come, My heart skips a beat when I think about our date together. Never forget that you were created to be passionately loved by Me like no other.

"You have captured My heart forever!"

Luke 23:46

Prayer:

Jesus, this touches my heart with Your love. It truly is the desire of my heart to know Your passionate love for me. I want You to be my first love forever. I want to come closer. I want to sit in Your presence and be so close that I feel Your breath on me as You whisper Your loving words to me. I pray that I will feel Your burning passionate love for me right now as I spend time with my lover. In Your precious name, Amen.

If it is your heart's desire, spend some time crying out to Jesus with all of your heart that you want Him to be your first love. Picture yourself melting in His arms and let Him take your breath away. Love on Him and then let Him love on you. Listen to His precious words of love for you. Rest in His arms awhile until you let Him truly take your breath away with His love. Be transformed in His presence. Journal whatever is on your heart.

~Day 66~

I DO NOT COUNT YOUR SINS AGAINST YOU!

"Beloved, I know the worst sin you will ever do in your life, and yet I still say, 'You are the one I want.' I know every time you lose your temper, get jealous, grow impatient, etc. I know every sin you have and will ever commit, even the secret ones you are too ashamed to admit. Yet, I tell you that you are the one I want. I chose you to be Mine forever.

"My precious child, do not wait to be perfect to receive My love and forgiveness for you. Do not wait! I want you to realize with all of your heart that I do not count your sins against you. I am not making a list of sins you commit and condemning you with it. If you believe I am making a list, I want you to know that this is a lie of the enemy that you are believing. I remind you over and over again, beloved, Jesus took all of your sin on the cross because of His love for you. You were chosen to be in My Kingdom forever!

"My love, you do not have to pay for your sins any longer in My eyes. You may have to deal with earthly consequences and repent to others for the hurt you have caused them, however, you have been completely reconciled to Me through My precious Son. Because of His shed blood and becoming your sin on the cross, I never, ever count your sins against you, no never! When you truly receive this revelation in your heart, it will transform you from the inside out.

"Come, let Me give you a revelation of what the cross means for you right now. Ask Me to give you a revelation of the cross. You are living under a New Covenant of love, precious child. You are the one I want to spend eternity with!"

Ephesians 1:4; 2 Corinthians 5:19, 21; Matthew 5:23-24; 1 Corinthians 2:2

Prayer:

Thank You for reminding me, Heavenly Daddy, that You do not count my sins against me because of what Jesus did on the cross. Help this truth to sink deep into My spirit. Daddy, I desire a much deeper revelation of the cross in my life. Thank You for more revelation, Your love gift to me. In Jesus' name, Amen.

*Get rid of all guilt and shame if you are still carrying any and ask Jesus to help you overcome any struggles by His Spirit.

Spend some time thanking Jesus for your total forgiveness.

~Day 67~

SAY THE PRECIOUS NAME OF JESUS!

"Child, when you are feeling sad, say the name of Jesus out loud and see what happens. Precious one, when anxiety is attacking you and you don't know what to do, say the precious name of Jesus and feel the fear melt away. When someone has wounded you and you are hurting, say the name of Jesus and feel the pain leave. When you have failed and the enemy attacks you with guilt and condemnation, say the precious name of Jesus and feel those things disappear. When you are faced with a hopeless situation or diagnosis, beloved, say the precious name of Jesus and feel the peace that comes from Him. There is so much power in the name of Jesus.

"Lift up the name of Jesus. Give glory to the name of Jesus. Worship Jesus and see what happens in your life. Say it right now from your heart. Say, 'Jesus. Jesus. Jesus. You are so precious to me, Jesus. Jesus. Jesus. Jesus. Thank You for healing me, Jesus. Jesus. Jesus. Jesus. Thank You for saving me and redeeming my life from the pit. Jesus. Jesus. Jesus. I love You, Jesus. I love You, Jesus. I love You, Jesus.' Say it until peace comes upon you. Say it until the fear goes. Say it until you feel His love for you. Say the precious name of Jesus. There is no other name like the name of Jesus. There is no other Savior like Jesus. There is no one who compares to Jesus. There is no other love that goes beyond the love of Jesus. Call on Jesus right now and watch what happens. Call on Jesus and feel His glory upon you, in you, all over you. There is no other more glorious name than the precious name of Jesus. Whisper His sweet name right now. Whisper 'Jesus, Jesus, Jesus,' and wait for His joy to fall on you."

Philippians 2:9-11

Prayer:

I lift up Your name, sweet Jesus. There is none that compares to You. Thank You, Jesus, that I am seated with You right now in Heavenly places. Jesus, Your name is power. Jesus, there is love in Your name. Jesus, there is healing in Your name. Jesus, there is miracle breakthrough in Your name. Jesus, sweet Jesus, I love You. Jesus, You are everything to me. Jesus, You are grace and mercy. Jesus, I need You with every ounce of my being. Jesus, I need You now. Jesus, I love You.

*Continue worshipping Jesus in your own words and feel His tender heart of love towards you as He is touched by your worship.

Finish this: Jesus is...

_____

_____

_____

_____

_____

_____

_____

_____

_____

_____

_____

_____

_____

_____

_____

_____

_____

~Day 68~

I LONG TO BE INTIMATE WITH MY BRIDE

"My bride, My beautiful, precious bride, My heart aches to be your first love. My love for you is as far as the East is from the West. My love for you is more than every drop of water in all the oceans. My love for you is greater than the number of stars in the sky and even surpasses the grains of sand on the earth. My love for you is so wide, so deep, so long, so unending that it will take you an eternity to discover it.

"Come, let Me show you the deep, deep, passionate love I have for My bride. You are radiant before Me. I see you as holy and blameless in My sight because of the blood I shed for you. You are shining, radiant, and beautiful to Me. I have chosen you to be My bride forever.

"My bride, My precious bride, will you let Me have this dance? I am looking intently in your eyes, and I am pleased with what I see. I love you and nothing will ever change that. Come, let Me waltz with you. You will never be the same. Let's get to know each other intimately while we are dancing together. I love dancing with My precious bride."

Song of Solomon 4:1, 7; Ephesians 3:18; Colossians 1:22

Prayer:

Father, sometimes I don't feel like I am Your beautiful, precious bride. Father, give me a revelation of how You see me. Give me a deep revelation of how wide, how deep is the love of Christ that Paul prayed I would know in the book of Ephesians. Daddy, I want to know You more intimately, and I accept Your invitation today to get to know You more intimately. I was created for intimacy with You. Thank You, Daddy, that Your opinion of me never changes, not even when I fail. Bring me into deeper intimacy with You today. In Jesus' name, Amen.

*If possible, spend some time listening to quiet worship music and receive Daddy's love and whatever else He wants to pour into you. Picture yourself waltzing in Jesus' arms.

Spend some time writing about what it means to you to be Jesus' bride.

_____

_____

_____

_____

_____

_____

_____

_____

_____

_____

_____

_____

_____

_____

_____

_____

_____

_____

_____

_____

~Day 69~

FUN ADVENTURES WITH JESUS

I saw a vision of Jesus. I was with Him. I saw both of us on a roller coaster. We were having so much fun together. He was laughing and screaming with me. We were having such a blast. We both had our hands in the air as we were laughing hysterically. I could see our hair blowing in the wind. The roller coaster was going fast and moving up and down in certain places like a typical track would. Whenever the roller coaster went through a scary part, Jesus would cover my eyes and wrap His arms around me. When the scary part was over, He would take his hands off my eyes and smile and laugh with me. It was a touching vision that I will never forget. Picture yourself in the roller coaster with Him. He says to you:

"I love to have a blast with My children. I long for them to know that life with Me is not boring. If you are struggling with boredom, it is because you do not yet know Who I really am. Let Me show you Who I am. I love to have fun like you do. It was I Who put that desire to have fun in you when I created you. I want to have a blast with all of you. I am not boring. I am filled with joy and laughter, and I long to share that part of Myself with all of you. It grieves Me when many of My children are so serious in My presence thinking that they have to act a certain way in order to please Me. No, I long for you to relax and have fun with Me. Beloved, when you discover how fun I am to be around, you will want to spend more time with Me than anyone else. I enjoy to make My children not only laugh, but laugh hysterically!

"Child, there will be struggles in this life, represented by the scary parts on the roller coaster. Remember during those times that I am helping you through them, wrapping My arms of love around you. There are seasons of trials, but I do not leave you through them. Did you know that we can even have fun together during trials? Try it. Let Me show you. There is an adventure waiting for you the next time a trial comes your way. Let Me help you laugh your way to victory! I can help you to have joy and peace through the trials. Come to Me and let Me show you. Let's laugh together!

"Beloved, I want you to think of your life as a series of fun adventures with Me. You will have so much joy when you discover Who I am and what I have planned for you. In fact, you cannot even imagine how much fun I have waiting for you in Heaven. We are going to have a blast together forever.

"Come, let's have fun together today. Let Me show you what I have planned so that we can enjoy the day. I am ready for an adventure with you, My beloved."

Day 69 ~ Fun Adventures With Jesus

Psalm 2:4; Psalm 16:11; Luke 10:21; Ecclesiastes 3:4; Zephaniah 3:17

Prayer: Jesus, thank You so much for that touching picture. I can't wait to see how much fun we will have together today. I wonder what You have planned for me. I feel like a kid in a candy store, I am so filled with excitement. In Your name, Amen.

*Start to keep a journal of all the fun times with Jesus and write down things He does or says that makes you laugh. Get that journal out whenever you are struggling. As you keep track of the times He makes you laugh, watch them increase and continue to write them down. Share with people how funny Jesus is so that others can get to know who He truly is, the King of Joy!

~Day 70~

SEE THE WORLD THAT I CREATED JUST FOR YOU

"My dear, precious child, I want you to notice some things around you so that you understand in a profound way how much I love you. I am overwhelmed with love for you, My beloved.

"Precious one, do you see the butterflies and the rainbows? Do you see the snow on the mountains or the waves in the oceans? Have you noticed how many different animal species I created? Do you see the variety of trees I made and the different leaves that change colors during different seasons? Or how about a bare tree that gets covered in ice and sparkles during a wintry sunny day? It looks beautiful. I want you to know that I created all of this just for you. If you were the only one on the earth, I would have still created it all for your pleasure.

"Do you see the different colorful flowers I made? How about the rose? Do you sometimes smell their beautiful fragrance? I made that smell just for you. Do you see their delicate petals? I made them all for you to show you My intense love for you. Child, I want you to get a rose and smell it. Consider it a gift from Me to you. I want the rose to remind you of how much I adore you. Beloved, a rose symbolizes love. It is usually given as a gift to people who love each other. However, I have not only given you a rose, I have given you all of My creation on the earth for you to enjoy. It's all for your pleasure. My treasure, I created it just for you!

"Beloved, I want you to see My love for you when you take a nature walk or even go to the store and see all the colorful fruits and vegetables I made for you. I thought about it all before I made it. I reflected on how much I wanted you to enjoy all of My creation. See My love for you in a new way when you look at the world I made just for you!"

Genesis 1

Prayer:

Heavenly Daddy, I want to thank You today for all that You created for me: the trees, the flowers, animals, the oceans, fruits and vegetables, all the colors I see. Thank You that You loved me so much that You wanted to give me the best. Help me to understand Your love for me when I enjoy Your creation. In Jesus' name, Amen.

Spend some time thanking Heavenly Daddy for all the things you enjoy that He created for you. Write them down.

~Day 71~

THERE IS NO GREATER POWER THAT EXISTS THAN MY POWERFUL LOVE

"Beloved, you know how you felt during the best day of your life? You felt so much joy. You felt so much peace. You didn't want the day to end because of the ecstasy you were feeling. Remember that? Well, I want to share something with you. That feeling you had doesn't even compare to how I felt when I thought of you before the foundation of the world. I had so much joy thinking about how I wanted to create you. I was so happy to pick out a unique destiny for you. It brought Me so much pleasure to form you in your mother's womb and to bring you into this world.

"Child, earthly words cannot describe how much I love you and how I feel about you. I have the power to create anything I want to. I have the power to destroy anything I want to. I have the power to hold the universe in my Hand. I have the power to do every possible miracle. Yet I tell you that those powers are nothing compared to the powerful love I have for you. There is so much power in My love. When you get a glimpse of this powerful love, you will be filled with all the power you need to perform miracles in My name. My power will flow out of you unto others. My power in you will help set the captives free, and they will get a glimpse of My love for them. People are set free by My love. They need to know My love. I long for every person on the earth to get a revelation of the powerful love I have for them. If they only knew how much I loved them, they would stop believing the lies the enemy tells them about Who I am. They would stop seeing Me as a God who causes bad things to happen to them when they fail. That is a total lie from the kingdom of darkness. My people need to know My love.

"Child, spread the news. Spread the news that I am a good Daddy, and I love My children with an unending, powerful love. Let the truth be known so that My people can be free."

Jeremiah 1:5; Isaiah 44:2; Ephesians 1:4; 3:17-18

Prayer:

Heavenly Father, I am so amazed at how much You love me and how You felt about me even before I was created. Let this truth go deep into my spirit to set me completely free. Give me this revelation so that I can share this wonderful news with others. In Jesus' name, Amen.

*Try to tell someone today how much Jesus loves them.

Write a letter to your Heavenly Daddy telling Him why He is so good. Tell Him how much you want to experience His powerful love.

~Day 72~

STANDING IS EASY WHEN YOU KNOW WHO YOU ARE!

"I call you My beloved. Do you know that your identity is in being My cherished, beloved child. You are My beloved. I do not call the devil or his kingdom 'My beloved' because they have chosen to leave My Kingdom and all of My blessings. Now, they are powerless, and all they live for is trying to deceive My children out of their inheritance and destiny. The enemy knows that when you get a revelation that you are My beloved, you are able to easily stand against all the lies that he feeds you to try to make you as powerless and miserable as he is. The only power he has is the power that you give to him when you believe his lies.

"Child, I want you to really know who you are. I want you to know without a shadow of a doubt that I see you as righteous as My Son because of what He willingly did for you on the cross. I want you to really know that I see you as the head and not the tail. I see you as an important part of My Kingdom. I see you as My child whom I love so much and brought into this world to love on. I see you as royalty! I see the destiny I have for you, and I want you to walk into it. I want you to realize that my glory lives in you because I am there. Wherever you go, you bring Heaven to earth. You are a light shining in the darkness. I want you to realize this. I want you to realize how much you change the atmosphere when you walk into a room. I want you to realize who you are so that it is not tiring work to stand against the enemy. I want you to realize how defeated that kingdom is. He who is in you is greater than he who is in the world! When you understand this, you will no longer let him rob you of anything that belongs to you. When you understand this, you will even take back what he stole and make him repay you seven times more! Know who you are!

"Child, start looking up Scriptures that tell you who you are in Me, and start speaking them out loud, and let these truths sink into your heart and your spirit. The more you know who you are, the easier it is to stand and receive all the inheritance that is rightfully yours as My beloved child."

Ephesians 6:11; 2 Corinthians 5:21; Deuteronomy 28:13; 1 John 4:4; Joel 2:25

Prayer:

Dear Heavenly Daddy, thank You for reminding me how easy it is to stand against the kingdom of darkness when I realize my identity in Christ. Show me Scriptures You want me to meditate on so that this truth goes deep into my spirit. In Jesus' name, Amen.

Write down some Scriptures that talk about who you are in Christ. Meditate on them today.

~Day 73~

I BECAME FILTHY TO MAKE YOU CLEAN

I saw a vision of a woman. The woman lost her temper and said some things that she regretted to her children. She went and looked at herself in the mirror, and she saw herself with dirt all over her face. She saw herself as unclean, filled with guilt and shame over what she had done. She left the mirror with her head looking down. Jesus came over to her and tried to take her hand, but she said, "No Jesus, I am not clean before you."

Next, I saw this same woman gossiping about someone. When she was finished, she realized what she had done was wrong. When she looked in the mirror again, she saw herself covered in dirt. She felt very dirty. I saw this happen again and again but Jesus was always pursuing the woman to come to Him.

One day, the woman felt broken enough that she took Jesus' hand as He was holding it out to her. As they were hand in hand, Jesus gently walked her over to the mirror. When the woman looked in the mirror, she again saw herself as filthy and unclean and wanted to run out of the room, but Jesus wouldn't let her. He said, "No, let Me show you something." As she looked in the mirror, she saw a vision in the mirror of Jesus enduring the cross. She saw Him walking with the cross on His back. She saw Him bending over from the weight of the cross, about to collapse. As she saw this happening, Jesus was taking a wet cloth and washing her face off. As she saw the dirt disappearing off of her face, she would see the dirt appear on Jesus' face in the vision she was watching in the mirror. As Jesus continued to wash her face, as her face got cleaner and purer, Jesus' face became full of wounds, bloody, and filled with dust. He said this to her:

"My beloved, I washed you clean that day. I took all of your filth. I took all of your sin. I took it all upon myself to make you clean. You have been washed white as snow, My beloved. Your conscience has been washed clean by My blood. Because of what I have done, you can come boldly to Me.

"Let Me show you how much I love you. Let Me show you that I have freed you from guilt and shame. Do not let the enemy condemn you with any sins you have committed. Do not let Him deceive you into thinking that you are unclean and can no longer come into My presence. I tell you to come boldly into My presence and let Me show you what I did for you and how I truly see you. The truth is that it gave Me great joy to wash you completely clean. You are My precious, pure, clean bride that brings Me such happiness."

Day 73 ~ I Became Filthy To Make You Clean

Hebrews 4:16; 10:22; Isaiah 1:18; Ephesians 3:12; 5:25-27; Colossians 1:22; Song of Solomon 4:7

Prayer:

Jesus, thank You for washing me white as snow. Thank You for Your amazing love and for making me forever clean with Your precious blood. I love You, Jesus. I love You. I glorify Your name. In Your name, Amen.

*Whenever you wash your face, let that be a reminder to you that Your Savior has washed you white as snow. Picture Jesus getting all dirty and dusty as He endured the suffering of the cross. Meditate on Him becoming filthy to make you clean. Start praising Him!

Journal about what this vision means to you.

~Day 74~

I LOVE IT WHEN YOU COME TO ME LIKE A CHILD!

I saw a vision of a little girl running and jumping into her father's arms. They were both filled with joy. I then heard these words:

"I absolutely love it when My children come to Me like little children. I love it when they come to Me, say whatever is on their mind, and ask Me for what they need with vulnerability and no fear. It brings Me such happiness when My children trust Me enough to let Me hold them. I love it when they run to Me instead of hide.

"Little children who are not wounded trust their daddy will take care of them. They trust that they are not bothering their daddy when they need and want affection. Beloved, I want you to come to Me like this. Come to Me with your needs. Come to Me when you need love and affection, and I will meet that need. Start trusting that I am the Father Whom you have been waiting for. I can fill all of your father and mother voids. I am the only parent who will never hurt you or wound you. I so desire for you to draw from Me and not be afraid. I absolutely love to meet your needs and desires. You can trust Me. Do not be afraid to come to Me. I tell you to come boldly to Me and tell Me what you need. Come to Me like a child, and I will take care of you. Let Me take care of the needs you did not have met as a child. Let Me show you that I am a good Father and I love you unconditionally for all eternity."

Matthew 19:13-15; 20:28; Hebrews 4:16; Ephesians 3:12; Psalm 116:6

Prayer:

Heavenly Daddy, I am so in awe of how much You love me and want to take care of me. You are truly the Daddy I have dreamed of having my whole life. I pray that I would know You even more as my precious Daddy. Help me to come boldly to You in my time of need. Help me to come boldly to You when I need You to love on me. Help me to be like a little child and run into Your arms of love. Thank You so much for the joy I have in knowing You love me so much. Thank You for being My Daddy. In Jesus' precious name, Amen.

*Keep saying out loud, "I can go boldly to My Daddy anytime I want to, even when I fail, because of what Jesus did for me." Picture yourself running into His arms like a little child and letting Him love you. Receive His loving embrace.

Write about what it means to come to Daddy like a child.

~Day 75~

WILL YOU JUMP IN THE RIVER?

I saw a vision of Jesus in a river. In the river, I saw lots of little children swimming around and having a blast. I saw some children out of the river on the bank, hesitating about whether or not to jump in. Next, I saw Jesus in the river next to the bank. His arms were held out as He was trying to persuade a child to jump into His arms to come into the river. He was very loving and reassured the child that it would be fun. That child refused to come in, and Jesus was grieved. However, He moved to the next child and that child didn't hesitate, jumped in His arms, and Jesus was full of bliss. He again tried to talk the other child into coming in again, always pursuing this child, but the child refused. Jesus did not want this child to miss out on all of the fun, but He did not force the child to come in. In the meantime, all the children that went in with Jesus were full of joy and having so much fun in the river and in His presence. I heard these words:

"Child, there is a river that flows from the throne of Heaven to the earth. This river carries My presence. This river refreshes My children. This river produces joy in My children. This river gives peace to My children. There is healing in this river. This river satisfies their every need and gives life. This river carries the glory they have desired. I want all of My children to experience this river. I want them to be so completely immersed in the rivers of living water that they will never dry out or thirst again. I do not ever force anyone to be with Me, but I am always pursuing them with My love and the good things that I want to give them. Child, when you jump into this river, you will never want to leave it. You will experience joy like never before. You will be overflowing with joy and laughter. I love to see My children laughing with the joy of the Holy Spirit. Laughter comes from Me!

"Precious one, when you jump into this river, you will experience Jesus and all that He is. Jesus is the way to this river. Picture yourself with Jesus right now. He is holding His arms out to you. What will you do? Come, be filled with joy, peace, healing, and the glory. Jesus is waiting for you."

Revelation 22:1

Prayer: Jesus, I am coming into Your presence right now to be refreshed. Thank You for being my living water. You are so precious. In Your name, Amen.

*See yourself jumping into Jesus' arms, see what He shows you, and be blessed! Say whatever is on your heart. Give Him praise. Worship Him. Love on Him and feel your joy increase.

Journal whatever is on your heart after reading today's devotional.

_____

_____

_____

_____

_____

_____

_____

_____

_____

_____

_____

_____

_____

_____

_____

_____

_____

_____

_____

_____

_____

~Day 76~

I LOVE IT WHEN YOU DANCE LIKE LITTLE CHILDREN

I saw a vision of a church. I heard a fast-playing worship song in the background. I saw that most of the people were bored, some were even yawning, some were looking at their watches wondering when the service was going to end, and most people were untouched. Next, I saw Jesus come and try to liven up the worship by getting some people to raise their hands, but they didn't notice Him, and as He tried to lift their arms, they resisted.

Next, I saw a vision of people worshiping in a different church. I heard the song "Undignified" playing. All of the people were dancing, jumping up and down, waving their hands in the air, waving banners, running around, totally letting loose. I saw Jesus with them. I will tell you that He was the one that was the most "undignified" dancing with them. He was having so much fun with His children. He had His hands raised in the air and was waving them all around. He had a big smile on His face and was filled with joy. I heard Him say these words:

"I love it when My children let loose and worship Me with all that they have. I love it when they dance like little children having fun with their Daddy. It pleases Me so much and makes My heart skip a beat.

"Beloved, there are times when you waltz with your lover and you gaze into each other's eyes with love. However, there are times when you let loose with your lover and just have fun because of the love you share together. My children, it is no different with Me. I love to waltz with you and gaze into your beautiful eyes. Yet, I also love to let loose and dance like an excited child and have fun with you. Do you think it is any different for Me? I love having fun with My Father. The only ones that find this kind of worship foolish are the ones that don't truly know Me or My Father. They are missing out on so many blessings. It grieves Me to see them miss out.

"Come to Me like a little child, and you will be blessed beyond your wildest dreams. Little children are free to be who they are with no fear. Child, I want the same for you.

"Precious one, if you are lacking joy, come, let loose. Let your worship break off the spirit of heaviness. The devil can't stand it when you are having fun. He flees! He can't stand to be in the presence of joy. Come! Let My oil of joy fall on you and set you free."

Psalm 30:11; Psalm 149:3; Psalm 150:4; Ecclesiastes 3:4; Jeremiah 31:13; Mark 10:13-16

Day 76 ~ L Love It When You Dance Like Little Children

If you have a hard time dancing in worship and the desire of your heart is to change that, say this prayer:

Jesus, I would like to let loose and worship You with all of my heart, but I have walls up that are preventing me. Would You ignite my heart with Your passionate love so strongly that I will just have to let loose and worship You with song and dance no matter who is around me? That is the desire of my heart. Thank You for helping me, Jesus. Thank You for loving me that much. In Your precious name, Amen.

*If possible, play the song "Undignified" (info at www.davidcrowderband.com) and dance like a child before your Daddy. Otherwise, find a fun, dancing worship song and dance like you have never danced before and feel the joy come.

Journal about what it means to you to dance and let loose like a child before the Lord.

~Day 77~

SOAK UP THE SON!

I saw a vision of Jesus. He was like the sun shining in the sky. I could see the rays all around Him. He was shining down on the earth. He was bright, on fire, and full of light. I saw people on the earth. Those who looked up at Him and kept Him in their gaze with Him alone as their focus, their hearts became ignited. I saw their hearts start on fire. Their hearts were burning for Him. Experiencing Jesus' passionate burning love is what ignited these peoples' hearts on fire for Him. Those whose hearts were on fire became very noticeable on the earth. They were bright and shining, and people were asking, "What's different about these people? They are so filled with joy and peace. What is going on? I want what they have." Next, I heard Jesus say these words:

"When you keep your eyes focused on Me, you cannot help but feel My passionate burning love for you. I want you to soak up My love. I want you to soak it up. I want you to experience My burning passion for you, My beloved. Keep your eyes on Me. Keep your focus on Me. Never leave My gaze, and you will never doubt My love for you. The enemy tries many things to get your focus off of Me. He knows that you are victorious when you keep your focus on Me. He sees you radiant with My glory when you keep your eyes on Me. He sees your heart burn with passion when you keep your eyes on Me, and he hates it. Keep watch and look for the subtle ways he tries to distract you from My passionate eyes of fire.

"Precious one, come, soak up the Son. Come, let Me ignite your heart with a burning, passionate love for not only Me, but everyone around you. Come, let Me set you on fire with my fiery love. You will never, ever be the same. You will never want to leave My gaze again. Come, let Me warm you up. Come, My love is just what you need. Come, be in My presence. Come, I am always waiting for you. I love to love on you. I love it when you gaze up at My face so that I can see your beautiful eyes looking at Me. You are My beautiful bride that I adore."

Hebrews 12:2; Matthew 17:2; Psalm 141:8; 1 Corinthians 2:2

Prayer: Jesus, I want to get rid of all distractions that keep Me from focusing on You. Give me a hunger that can only be satisfied when I am focused on You. Jesus, ignite my heart with Your passionate, burning love so that I can spread it to others. I long to experience it right now. In Your precious name, Amen.

*Picture yourself gazing at Jesus' face all day and feel Him burning for you.

Write a letter to Daddy telling Him what it means to you to keep your eyes focused on Jesus. Tell Him you want a heart that burns for Him.

~Day 78~

I WILL NEVER BREAK YOUR HEART!

I was feeling pain one day over some rejection. The Lord gave me a vision as I was crying out to Him. I saw a picture of a heart lying on the ground. The heart was being kicked. The heart was being stabbed. The heart was being beaten. All of this symbolized some of the pain my heart has felt during my lifetime. Then, I saw Jesus pick up the battered, lifeless heart in His hands. He carefully picked the heart up and kissed it. He caressed it ever so gently. He wiped off all of the dirt. Next, I saw that the heart looked brand new with no wounds on it. He placed the new heart back inside of me to symbolize that His love is what will heal all of the rejection wounds I have had in my life. Picture Him doing this with your heart.

Next, I heard Him say, "My beloved child, it saddens Me to see the pain you have been through in your life. Rejection from others was never a part of My plan, and I see how it has wounded your heart. I see how you are afraid to share your heart with others. I see how you have fear of being vulnerable with others for fear of being hurt. Precious one, I want you to know that you can always be vulnerable with Me, and I will never, ever reject you. I will never, no never break your heart! You never have to worry about how you come across with Me. I know everything about you. I care about you in a deep, deep way, and I will never hurt you. I want you to share your pain, your concerns, your cares, and your worries with Me. I don't want you to ever be afraid to share what is on your heart with Me, ever! Nothing will ever change the way I feel about you, no nothing! You will always be My beloved, precious child. I am so saddened to see the pain you have been through in your life. Let Me heal all of the sadness and brokenness you have been through. Let Me take away your fear of rejection. Give it to Me, and I will set it at the foot of the cross because that is where it belongs. My Son carried all of your sorrows at the cross. Child, give them all to Me and let Me do a deep inner healing in your heart and soul. Let Me take that battered heart and make it new. Let Me kiss it with My love. I care deeply about you. Rest assured, I will never, ever break your heart or hurt you. You can trust Me, My beloved."

Isaiah 53:5; 1 Peter 5:7

Prayer: Jesus, thank You for healing my broken heart. Thank You for taking all of my pain and healing all of my wounds. You are my healer. Thank You for never rejecting me. In Jesus' name, Amen.

 *Picture Jesus picking up your broken heart, wiping the dirt off, kissing it, and healing it. Thank Him.

Share any rejection wounds you have with your Daddy. Tell
Him that you want to give it all to Him right now.
Write about what this vision means to you personally.

_____

_____

_____

_____

_____

_____

_____

_____

_____

_____

_____

_____

_____

_____

_____

_____

_____

_____

_____

_____

_____

~Day 79~

JUST ONE DROP OF MY BLOOD

The Lord reminded me of an experiment I used to do as a child. (If you can do this experiment, do it now and then read the following words). I filled a bowl with water. Then, I sprinkled some pepper in the water and saw it floating all over the top of the water. I put one drop of dishwashing soap in the center of the bowl on the pepper and saw all of the pepper immediately rush to the edges of the bowl. Then, the Lord showed me a vision. I saw Jesus in the heavens. I saw His head, and it was huge and over the entire world. I saw the crown of thorns on His head. His head was looking down. He had just given up His Spirit on the cross. I saw one huge drop of blood fall down to the earth. I saw this drop of blood fall onto hospitals. As soon as the blood hit the hospitals, all the people rushed out of the hospital (like the pepper) and came out healed. I saw this drop of blood fall onto psychiatric hospitals, nursing homes, and everywhere that the sick were. When the drop would fall, crowds of people in those places would come out immediately healed. I heard these words:

"Just one drop of My blood is enough for the entire world to be completely healed, delivered, and set free. I long for My children to get this revelation. I long to see My people completely healed. I paid the price for their healing. I love them so much. I want them to experience the abundant life I came to give them. I came to give life and life to the full.

"Precious one, if you are sick, picture one drop of My blood falling on you right now. Picture yourself healed as the tiniest part of the drop hits you. Sickness flees when it sees the blood. It cannot stay. Let Me give you this revelation. Let this go from your head to your heart. You are qualified to receive My healing. Let this truth sink deep into your spirit. I paid for your healing because of My deep, deep love for you. It pains Me to see you suffer. Come to Me, let Me comfort you, and let this revelation heal you. You are so precious to Me, and healing is your inheritance. Receive it, child. Receive it. It is my gift to you."

Isaiah 53:5; Jeremiah 33:3; Mark 16:18; Psalm 103:3

Prayer:

Jesus, thank You so much for paying for my healing. Thank You for this powerful vision which shows me the power of Your blood. Thank You for shedding Your precious blood for my complete emotional and physical healing. Show me that I am qualified to receive healing. Show me what lies I am believing that are preventing me from receiving. Help me replace all lies with the truth. In Your name, Amen.

If you can, do the experiment described before the vision. Then, think about what this means to you and journal your thoughts to Daddy. Thank Jesus for shedding His precious blood for your healing.

~Day 80~

MY CROWN OF THORNS FOR YOUR ROYAL CROWN

I saw a vision of Jesus with the crown of thorns on His head. He was in a lot of pain as the thorns were digging deep into His flesh. I remembered the Scripture that talked about one of the soldiers beating Jesus on the head when He had the crown of thorns on. I saw Jesus in so much pain, and blood started to pour from His head all over His body. Next, I saw a vision of Jesus putting a royal, golden crown on all of His people. Then I heard these words:

"My precious child, I took the crown of thorns on My head to give you peace of mind. Whenever the kingdom of darkness comes in with evil, negative, hopeless, or racing thoughts, remember that I won your peace of mind. I won the battle for you. I purchased a royal crown for you that day. You belong to My Kingdom. Take authority over your mind in My name and start thinking on thoughts above. See that rod that I was beaten with as a royal staff in your hand because I have given you authority over all the power of the enemy." I immediately saw a picture of a woman taking the staff and lifting it up high, and, as soon as demons saw it, they started to flee. Then the Lord said:

"You belong to My Kingdom and peace is your inheritance. Precious one, any time you start to feel down or depressed, start going back to what thoughts were in your mind. What have you been dwelling on? Throw out all lies from the enemy and start meditating on the truth. See the crown of thorns on My head. I wore it for your freedom. Whenever you do not feel peace of mind, it's as if you are wearing a crown of thorns. Child, I want you to wear the crown I bought for you and placed on your head the moment you accepted Me into your life. Beloved, I love you so much, and it grieves Me to see you in anxiety and not peace. It grieves Me because of what I bought for you. I want you to receive peace of mind. I love you so much that I want you to cast all your cares and anxieties on Me and let Me carry them for you. I don't want you to carry them. Give them to Me, precious one. Do you see how much I love you?

"Child, picture yourself right now with a royal crown on your head and a staff in your hand that comes from Me. See yourself lifting the staff high and watching all mental torment flee. The enemy can't stand it when My children get a revelation of the authority I have given them over his pathetic kingdom."

John 19:2; Matthew 27:30; Colossians 1:13; 3:1-3, 15; Luke 10:19; 1 Peter 5:7

Prayer: Heavenly Daddy, today I am choosing to think on thoughts above and on the truth. I come against all mental assaults of the enemy in Jesus' name, and I receive the peace of mind that Jesus purchased for me. In His name, Amen.

Write down any lies that you have been believing and next to them, replace them with truth. Write down what it means to you that Jesus purchased your peace of mind.

~Day 81~

DO NOT BE AFRAID TO DRAW ANYTHING FROM ME

Some of you may find this funny, and it is. It is our Daddy's sense of humor. It is a fun vision, but very symbolic. I saw a vision of Jesus, and He was dressed in a waiter's outfit. He came up to a table of His children and said, "What can I get you today?" The people said, "Oh no, Jesus, let us serve you." He replied:

"No, I love it when you take from Me. Don't be afraid to draw anything from Me. The Son of man came to serve and not be served. I am here to serve you. I am so full of everything you need. I am like a well that never dries up.

"My beloved, I am always waiting for you to draw from Me. I love it when you draw from Me. Do you need healing? Draw healing from your healer. Do you need a supernatural debt cancellation? Draw prosperity from Me. Do you need a miracle? Draw that miracle from Me. Do you need patience? Draw patience from Me. Do you need some hope and encouragement? Take from Me. Do you need rest? Come, rest in Me and My love for you. I love it when you have the faith to believe that I enjoy rewarding those who diligently seek Me. My desire is to give to My children. I am a giver! I love it when you take from Me. I love it when you do not reverse the roles and feel like you have to work for Me in order to earn the gifts that I have for you. When you draw from Me, you will serve Me out of a heart of love and not obligation.

"Child, go into a quiet place. Put on some quiet worship music. Let Me fill you with what you need. Don't pray or worship during this time. Let Me fill you. I know you have a hard time receiving, but I long to break that lie from the enemy. Today, receive from Me. Draw from Me. Tell Me what you need and then quiet yourself and receive. I want you to get the revelation that it brings Me great joy to give to you and fill you with what you need. Receive this truth for your heart. I love you precious one. I am your Daddy Who wants to provide you with everything you need. Receive!"

Mark 10:45; Genesis 22:14; Hebrews 11:6

Prayer: Jesus, help me to not be afraid to draw from You whatever I need to get me through each day. I can't do anything without You and without drawing what I need from You. I pray that I will be refreshed as I draw from Your presence in the secret place today. In Your name, Amen.

*Let Jesus love on you right now. Surrender yourself into His loving arms.

Spend some time writing Jesus a letter telling Him what you need to draw from Him. Share your heart with Him.

_____

_____

_____

_____

_____

_____

_____

_____

_____

_____

_____

_____

_____

_____

_____

_____

_____

_____

_____

Day 81 ~ Do Not Be Afraid To Draw Anything From Me

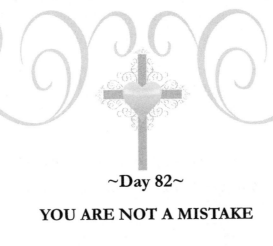

~Day 82~

YOU ARE NOT A MISTAKE

"Dear one, you know how a parent feels when he sees his child born? Or when a parent adopts a child and sees him for the first time? That parent thinks, 'Wow, this is my precious child. I can't wait to watch him grow up. I can't wait to do things with him. I can't wait to love on him. I can't wait to take care of him and provide for all of his needs. I can't wait to have fun with him. I can't wait until I hear the words from his mouth, "I love you Daddy." I can't believe he is mine.' Precious one, this is how I felt about you. When you came into the world, I thought those same things! I have been watching you grow up, and I continue to watch you. I rejoiced the day you started walking. I rejoiced the day you started talking. I have recorded every first event for you in My heart. Your baby book is and will always be in My heart!

"Some of you did not have earthly parents that represented Me to you. They did not feel this same way about you. You were created to have earthly parents that felt this way about you. However, the enemy has unfortunately stolen this from many of My precious children. Let Me tell you, it grieves Me to see My children neglected, abandoned, and abused. It grieves Me to no end. It absolutely breaks My heart. You were created to be loved on not only by Me, but also by your earthly parents. That was My desire and plan for your life from the beginning.

"Dear one, I want you to know that I sent My Son to take your sorrows, pain, and abuse on the cross. He took your broken heart on the cross. Beloved, He is the answer to all of this pain you have been carrying around from your childhood. The answer is not to dwell on the past, it is to keep your eyes focused on Jesus and what He did for you. It is to see that all that stuff was crucified on the cross with My Son. He took it and gave you all the healing you will ever need.

"Beloved, I want you to know that I can more than fill that void you feel that your earthly parents left. I want to be the Dad and Mom you always dreamed of. Let Me show you that I am proud of you and I am so glad you were made. You are not a mistake. I do not make mistakes! You are here for a purpose. Let Me show you what that purpose is, My beloved child."

Romans 8:16; Isaiah 53:4-5; Hebrews 12:2

*Say a prayer and then spend some time thanking Jesus for taking your childhood pain.

Write Daddy a letter telling Him that it is your heart's desire that He fill the void left by your earthly parents and thank Him for being the best parent you could ever have.

_____

_____

_____

_____

_____

_____

_____

_____

_____

_____

_____

_____

_____

_____

_____

_____

_____

_____

_____

~Day 83~

KICKING THE ENEMY OUT IS AS EASY AS 1, 2, 3!

I saw a vision of a woman, and she was full of anxiety, and her mind was racing. She put her hands on her head and was full of fear and torment. Next, I saw a vision of a demon taking a food mixer with beaters, and he plugged it in and turned it on inside her head. I realized that this demon was causing her to have a racing mind, anxiety, and torment. Finally, I saw Jesus appear. He told the woman to look at Him, and He said, "It's as easy as 1, 2, 3," and when He said, "3," He unplugged the mixer from the outlet and all the fear and torment stopped. Next, I heard Him say this:

"My beloved, I want you to use the authority I have given you. I tell you that I have given you full and total authority over ALL the power of the enemy. I purchased it for you at the cross. It is part of your inheritance. I want you to use it. I don't want you to remain powerless. I want you to use it. If you don't have a full revelation of this authority, ask Me for it. I will give it to you. It grieves Me to see My precious ones in torment.

"Child, I want you to renew your mind with My precious truths. Don't even entertain "what ifs." Those are not from Me. Don't let the enemy replay things in your mind over and over about certain situations. That is a huge tactic he uses to torment My children. Don't meditate on those useless thoughts. Instead, fill yourself with My life-giving words. Don't let the enemy get a foothold. Use your authority. It's easy. It's not complicated. Let Me show you how easy it is. Just picture how easy it was for Me to unplug the food mixer. Now, picture yourself with Me in that scene. I am now taking your hand and helping you to unplug it. I want you to picture this vision when the enemy tries to come in and torment your mind. Child, torment does not belong to you, rather My perfect peace belongs to you. Receive it, My beloved. Receive it. It pains Me to see My precious ones trampled by the enemy, and I don't want you to be one of them. I love you and want the best for you. That is why I have given you total authority over ALL the power of the enemy."

Luke 10:19; Colossians 2:15; Ephesians 4:26-27; 1 John 4:18; Isaiah 26:3; Psalm 90:13

Prayer: Jesus, thank You so much for reminding me that I am not meant to live a life filled with anxiety, fear, and torment. I vow to start using the authority that You have given me and to stop entertaining useless, life-sapping thoughts. Thank You for Your love for me. In Your precious name, Amen.

Look up today's Scripture verses and write about them.

_____

_____

_____

_____

_____

_____

_____

_____

_____

_____

_____

_____

_____

_____

_____

_____

_____

_____

_____

~Day 84~

MY FIERY LOVE IS ALREADY IN YOU!

"Child, whether you realize it or not, My fiery love is within you. The moment you said, 'I want to be yours,' I poured My fiery love inside of you. There is nothing that is hotter than My fiery love for you. You do not have to earn this love. It still burns within you no matter what you do or don't do. It is My gift to you.

"There is nothing that is hotter than my fiery love for you. Do you want freedom? There is nothing that my fiery love cannot burn up in your life. No addiction, no trauma, no rejection is too great for Me to burn up and heal in your life.

"Beloved, when you see the sun, what do you see? You see a bright shining star that is too bright for you to stare at for too long. You sometimes feel the intense heat that the sun brings. Child, the sun is extremely hot and on fire, and it is hottest at its center. Precious one, in the same way, when you make My Son the center of your life, you will feel His fiery, passionate love for you. You will be so on fire that everyone around you will notice it. You will cause a spark in those people you touch. My fiery love inside you will spread like wildfire around you and to your family. The enemy will try to extinguish it at times, but he will not succeed. Once My children truly feel My fiery, passionate love, there is no going back to the way they once lived. There is no going back to the emptiness they once felt. Those who experience My passionate love know without a doubt that it fills every single void that they have ever had. It is the only thing that fills every void.

"Let My fiery love within you consume everything that is not from Me. Let My fiery love set you free! Do you feel it? Come to Me, and I will show you what you already have."

Romans 5:5; Hebrews 12:29; Revelation 1:16; Deuteronomy 4:24

Prayer:

Jesus, I don't always feel Your passionate, fiery love for me, but I know that it is already within me. Please give me a deep revelation that Your love is more passionate than any love I could ever receive from anyone. Will You fill me with the fire of Your love today? In Your name, Amen.

*Thank Jesus for His fiery, passionate love for you and ask Him to let you experience it today in a deeper way. If the sun is out, feel the heat and picture His fiery love warming you up.

*Write a letter to Jesus telling Him what you want His fiery love
to burn off of you. Tell Him how much you need His fiery, passionate love.*

~Day 85~

I AM WITH YOU ALWAYS!

"Beloved, when you are looking in the mirror and brushing your hair or getting ready, I am looking in the mirror with you. I am gazing into your beautiful eyes at that very same moment. When you are sad, I am looking at you with eyes of comfort. When you are happy, I am smiling with you. I am with you through it all. I love looking at you! Child, even while you are brushing your teeth, I am with you, smiling at you the whole time. I am always with you!

"Precious one, while you are at the grocery store buying things that you need, I am still with you. I never leave you. I even sometimes whisper ideas to you of things that I know you enjoy to buy, and I even lead you to them. I am with you always!

"Child, while you are making dinner or watching TV, I am still with you. I am with you in everything you do. When you fully comprehend that I am always with you, it will change your life. Beloved, today, try to picture Me with you in everything you do. Give it a try, and you will be blessed, and we will fellowship together. I live in you and am with you always in every detail of your life. I love being with you every moment of every day!"

Matthew 28:20; Colossians 1:27

Prayer:

Jesus, thank You so much for reminding me that You are with me always in every little detail of my life. Help me to realize Your precious presence with me today in a special way. Help me to remember to fellowship with You and involve You in the small details of My life because You care for my every need. In Jesus' name, Amen.

*Thank Jesus throughout the day for being with you at all times. Acknowledge His presence with you and thank Him for caring about every detail of your life. Talk to Him while you are getting ready. Fellowship with Him while you make dinner. Bring Him into everything you do today and feel His sweet presence loving on you.

Write a letter to Jesus from your heart thanking Him for always being with you, every minute of every day. Thank Him for never leaving you.

~Day 86~

I ALWAYS LOOK AT YOU WITH EYES OF LOVE

I saw a vision of Jesus dying on the cross. I saw Him ripped to shreds. I saw Him gasping for breath. I saw dried blood, bruises, and shredded skin all over Him. He was in agony. Next, I saw people mocking Him. They were looking at Him on the cross, and they were shouting insults and mocking Him. As my heart was broken for Him, I heard these words:

"My precious child, nothing could ever separate you from My love. Even as I was in agony of mind, soul, and body as I was dying on the cross, I looked down at the people who were mocking Me with eyes of love and compassion. Yes, I even love those who hate Me with an everlasting love. They are blinded, and I am filled with love and compassion for them. Child, there is nothing you could ever do that would take away the burning, passionate love I have for you. I want you to see that, even at Calvary, I could have called on My Father to rescue Me from the cup I willingly endured, but I refused to call on Him because I thought of you. I was so filled with love for you that the thought of losing you was much more torture than what I endured that day! That is how much you mean to Me. I couldn't bear thinking about losing you. Child, now that you belong to Me, rest assured, I will not let anyone snatch you out of My embrace. You are and will always be My precious treasure. I always look at you with eyes of love. Let this revelation transform you from the inside out. When you understand this, you too will be able to look at anyone who wounds you, rejects you, or mocks you with My eyes of love through you."

Romans 8:38; John 18:11; John 10:29

Prayer:

Jesus, thank You so much for willingly enduring the cup of wrath for me. Thank You for taking my punishment. I could never thank You enough. Thank You for Your passionate love that never dies. You are so precious to me. I lift up Your name, precious Jesus. I praise You, Jesus. You are so worthy to be praised and adored. To You be all the glory and honor and praise! Precious Jesus, thank You for transforming me with Your burning love. In Your name, Amen.

*Spend some time thanking Jesus for taking your cup of wrath. Tell Him how much this means to you. Thank Him for enduring extreme emotional and physical pain in order to set you free. Worship Him

Write a letter to Jesus about what is on your heart.

~Day 87~

YOU WILL FIND HIDDEN TREASURES IN MY WORD

"Beloved, I want to share so many secrets and revelations with you from My Word. I love it when My children seek Me for deeper revelation. There are so many hidden treasures just waiting for My people in the Word. I long to see My beloved children dig deep into My Word with hunger. I absolutely love it when My children are filled with extreme hunger for My Word. Beloved, if you do not have this hunger, ask Me for it. Seek Me for it, and I will give you a hunger that can only be satisfied when you are in My presence, reading My life giving words.

"The world has so many self-help books. These are distractions to take my people away from My Word. All of the answers to all of your problems are found in My Word.

"Child, the Bible is a gift to you. It is life! It is My love letter to you. If you seek My mysteries and secrets with all of your heart, you will find them. Are you ready to start a new adventure with Me?

"Come, go into the secret place and meditate on the Word. Let My words breathe life into you. I assure you, you will not be the same! Come, ask Holy Spirit to open up the mysteries to you as you read."

Jeremiah 29:13; Matthew 13:11; Joshua 1:8; Proverbs 25:2

Prayer:

Heavenly Father, I pray that You would give me a hunger for Your Word that cannot be satisfied until I am actually in the secret place reading it. I desire with all of my heart to know Your mysteries and secrets. I believe that those secrets are part of my inheritance. Holy Spirit, as I meditate on the Word, I pray that You would speak to me and tell me what I need to hear. Thank You for giving me the gift of Your Word and for opening up the mysteries to me. In Jesus' name, Amen.

*Ask Holy Spirit to highlight a verse for you today and ask Him for a deeper revelation of this verse. Ask Him to give you a new revelation in the Word and thank Him for it. Acknowledge His presence with you while you are reading the Word. Tell Him how much you love Him teaching you new things.

Spend some time thanking your Heavenly Father for the Word.
Tell Him what His Word means to you and how it has transformed your life.

~Day 88~

IT IS FINISHED!

I saw a vision. I heard Jesus say, "It is finished!" I saw and heard the veil being torn in two the moment Jesus willingly gave up His Spirit. After I saw the veil being torn in two, I immediately saw death certificates being torn in two. I heard, "It is finished." I saw medical diagnoses being torn in two. I heard, "It is finished." I saw bank debt notices being torn in two. I heard again, "It is finished." Next, I heard these words:

"Beloved, I want you to realize what I purchased for you with My own blood. I purchased eternal life. I defeated death for you. I purchased your complete healing of mind, soul, and body. I defeated sickness and disease for you. I purchased your prosperity. I defeated poverty and lack for you. I want you to know deep in your Spirit that I won all of this and so much more for you, My beloved. It is finished and done. The blessings are yours.

"I know that some of My children are frustrated. They have heard many teachings about this and even proclaim and decree Scriptures about these very same things. I tell you not to give up. Let Me show you what is blocking you from receiving your rightful inheritance. Child, let Me help you. Don't ever, ever give up hope. Don't ever think that I have abandoned you and that you are excluded from any blessings I tell you are yours in My Word. That is a lie from the enemy. He wants to keep you in doubt and unbelief. Precious one, I have so much compassion on you when I see how badly you want these promises to manifest in your life. I have so much compassion on you. Beloved, don't give up. Keep seeking Me. Let Me help you in your time of need. I tell you again, 'It is finished and done.' Let that sink into your spirit. Meditate on this vision and see things being finished. Child, they are finished in the spiritual realm. Reach out your hand in faith and take it. Take it in faith, precious one. Take it. Receive it.

"Beloved, you are so special and beautiful to Me. I have given you everything because of My great love for you. Meditate on this truth and let it sink in today."

John 19:30; Matthew 27:51; Mark 15:38; John 3:16; Isaiah 53:5; Ephesians 1:3; 2 Corinthians 8:9

Prayer: Jesus, thank You so much for becoming the curse for me and giving me every spiritual blessing. Jesus, I desire a deep revelation in my spirit that You finished everything for me and I can receive it because it is mine. Show me what is blocking me from receiving. In Your name, Amen.

*Write anything you struggle with on a piece of paper. Then, rip it in two and say, "Jesus finished this for me because He loves me." Praise Him!

Journal what you believe Jesus meant when He cried out,

"It is finished."

Ask Him to give you a deeper revelation of His finished work.

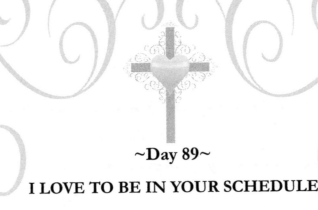

~Day 89~

I LOVE TO BE IN YOUR SCHEDULE

I saw a vision of a woman. She was a very busy woman that had a lot going on in her schedule. I saw her scheduling things on her cell phone calendar. Jesus was behind her and was looking at her screen. He said, "I wonder if she is going to schedule a date with Me." The woman had too many things in her schedule, and she did not schedule any time with Jesus. Then, I saw this woman throughout the day. Jesus went with her everywhere she went. When she was meeting a friend for coffee, Jesus was there with her, listening to her, and at one point He was even caressing her hair. Next, I saw her shopping, and Jesus was with her the whole time and He even had His arm in her arm, but the woman didn't realize it. Jesus was with her the whole time. I saw the woman exhausted at the end of the day. As she turned out the lights, Jesus gently kissed her on the cheek and said, "Goodnight, My love." Next I heard these words:

"My children, I love you so much. I love everything about you. I love spending time with you. I love you no matter what. I am always with you, loving on you whether you realize it or not. I love you so much. I know every detail about you. I know your schedule. I know how busy you are. I never leave you even when you forget about Me. This is true love. I love you no matter what. Nothing will ever change that.

"Beloved, because of how much I love and adore you and have your best interests at heart, I would love to see us fellowshipping together in your schedule. Beloved, come and be with Me before you start the busy day, and I will give you supernatural strength to meet all your needs. Precious one, if you write "Date with Jesus" on your planner everyday, you will see a change in your life. Child, give Me a chance. Let Me show you how much I love you, and I promise that you will want to be with Me instead of feeling like it is an obligation. You will start to hunger after Me, and you will want to put Me in your schedule more than once a day! Give Me a chance, and let My love cause you to fall deeper in love with Me. Beloved, even when you ignore Me, I still pursue you with My love, and I will never stop. You are always and forever in My schedule."

Romans 8:38-39

Prayer: Jesus, Your love continues to amaze me. Jesus, help me to realize that You are always with me throughout the day, no matter what my schedule brings. Jesus, prompt me to acknowledge Your presence and fellowship with You. Give me a hunger to want to be with You first thing everyday. In Your name, Amen.

Write Jesus a letter from your heart telling Him how it touched you that He said, "You are forever in My schedule."

~Day 90~

NOT GUILTY!

The Lord gave me a vision. It was of a woman who had just sinned. She felt major guilt, and the enemy was coming in with condemnation. She saw a courtroom. Satan came in the courtroom and pounded the gavel down and said, "Guilty!" The woman continued to feel guilt. She said to herself, "I am trying so hard not to commit this sin, but the enemy is right; I am guilty as charged." Then, Jesus showed her a vision. He showed her a vision of Him being nailed to the cross. Next, He showed her a vision of Him in the courtroom slamming down the gavel and saying, "Not guilty! Acquitted because I already paid the price." When He slammed the gavel down, it was full of His blood and the blood went all over the courtroom, sprinkling the woman and sprinkling the enemy. When the enemy felt the blood, he shrieked and left. When the woman felt the blood, she felt innocent, peaceful, and deeper in love with Jesus. He said these words:

"Whenever the enemy comes in with guilt and condemnation, remind yourself of what I did for you. Remind yourself that I acquitted you and no longer condemn you. Remind yourself that I did this because I love you. I want you to meditate on this and receive the love I have for you. When you receive My passionate love for you, you won't want to go out and sin. You will want to stay in My arms and feel My embrace. You will want to share with others the good news that I see them as 'not guilty' the moment they accept Me into their life.

"Precious one, get rid of all guilt and condemnation. See yourself the way I see you. You are so precious to Me. It pains Me when you are hard on yourself. It pains Me when you put expectations on yourself to be perfect. Child, I was perfect for you. Child, your imperfections are what made you realize you needed Me as your Savior. I am not hard on you. Please get rid of all thoughts of punishing yourself for not being perfect. Stop beating yourself up. It grieves Me when you allow your thoughts to go there. Beloved, start replacing those thoughts with My loving thoughts. Replace them with, 'My Jesus loves me so much that He not only became my sin, but He came to rescue me, set me free, make me a new creation, and bring me to be with Him forever.' That is the truth! I love you, precious one, just the way you are."

Psalm 103:3; Hebrews 8:12; Psalm 32:2; Romans 8:1; Romans 2:4

Prayer: Dear Jesus, thank You so much for becoming my sin, taking my punishment, and setting me free. Jesus, knowing You did this for me causes me to fall deeper in love with You instead of going out to sin some more. Thank You for Your unending grace in my life. In Your name, Amen.

Journal about what this vision means to you personally.
Did His words touch your heart? Why?

~Day 91~

I LOVE AN ATTITUDE OF GRATITUDE

"Child, I love it when you are filled with gratitude even during trials. I love it when you have a positive attitude. Gratitude shows Me that you trust Me in all things. The enemy constantly wants you to dwell on negative things. He is always reminding you about things you don't have. He always feeds you lies about why you shouldn't trust Me. He wants you to keep speaking negative, critical, life-sapping words. Negative words contradict faith-filled words. Remember, the power of life and death are in the tongue. When you focus on the negative, it only brings hopelessness, discouragement, and depression. This is not your inheritance! This is not the abundant life!

"Beloved, I want you to renew any negative thinking with truth and faith filled words. For example, instead of saying, 'I will never find a parking spot today,' say instead, 'I know the favor of My Heavenly Daddy is all over me. He loves to bless Me because He is so good. Daddy, I thank you in advance for the parking spot you have planned for me today. You care about the little things, even parking spots!' Do you see the difference? This is the difference between unbelief and faith.

"Child, I want you to receive the revelation that I am good and that I love you and want to prosper you. When you comprehend this in your heart, you will stand against doubt and unbelief. You will battle negative thinking and lies from the enemy. Start paying attention to any negative words that come out of your mouth. I will help you replace them with positive, life-giving words and truth. You will experience a new level of faith, joy, and peace when you really desire true change in your thinking and start doing this.

"Precious one, I am telling you this so that you will be blessed. I am telling you to have a grateful, positive attitude in order to go higher, which I know is the cry of your heart. I also want to remind you that My love for you does not change one bit when you speak negative words. I love you no matter what!"

James 1:2; John 8:44; Romans 12:2; Jeremiah 29:11; Proverbs 18:21; Psalm 100:4; 1 Thess. 5:18

Prayer:

Precious Heavenly Father, I want to change the negative thinking I have struggled with my whole life. I want to replace it with rejoicing and Kingdom thinking. I choose to renew my mind with Your loving, positive words, and I desire lasting change that will last the rest of my life. In Jesus' name, Amen.

*Anytime a negative thought comes to your mind, battle it with something positive. Keep reminding yourself that you are Heavenly Daddy's precious child and He has plans to prosper you and not harm you. Keep telling yourself, "My Daddy has good things planned for me everyday because He is so good."

Spend some time thinking about some negative attitudes the enemy puts in your mind. Write down some faith-filled words that battle those negative patterns of thinking.

~Day 92~

YOUR CHAINS CAME OFF THAT DAY!

I saw a vision. I saw many people with heavy chains on them. It was difficult for them to move or walk. Next, I saw Jesus the moment He was resurrected and immediately, I heard a very loud noise. I heard many, many chains dropping to the ground. This happened for quite awhile. The sound was very loud. As chains were dropping, I heard the sound of many demons screaming and fleeing. Next, I saw something that surprised me. I saw many of these same people. Their chains were gone in the Spirit, but they were walking and moving as if they still had chains on. Jesus saw this and started weeping. I heard these words:

"My precious, precious children, I want you to understand with all of your heart that I set you completely free at the cross. I removed your chains that day. I broke the curse that day. I set you free. Beloved, I want you to get a revelation that I have already set you free. I have given you the power to keep those chains off for good. I have given you all power and authority over all demons. When they try to put those chains back on you, tell them to get lost. Tell them, 'No, I have been set free by My Jesus because of His great love for me. He came to give me an abundant life. An abundant life is total freedom with no chains. This is my inheritance.'

Next, I saw a vision of Jesus. He was taking all of the chains that had fallen to the ground, and He was throwing them in the pit of hell. He said, "Those chains belong to the kingdom of darkness. I have translated you out of their kingdom into Mine. You are from another Kingdom. You are from the Kingdom of freedom! You are free! You have been set free! You are free indeed because of what I did for you. Receive it child. Take back what the enemy stole. Keep those chains off. Let Me help you. Call out to Me, and I will answer you. I want to see you walk in freedom, My beloved, I set you free to live. I set you free because of My burning love for you."

Isaiah 61:1; John 8:36; Colossians 1:13; John 10:10; 2 Corinthians 3:17

Jesus, thank You for setting me free. Thank You for giving me an abundant life. Thank You for freedom! Thank You for wanting me completely free! Jesus, show me what is blocking me from receiving the revelation that You have set me completely free. Show me any lies that I am believing so I can replace them with the truth. I proclaim that Jesus has set me totally free. I will continue to let this truth sink deep into My spirit. My chains are gone! Hallelujah! In Your name, Amen.

Write down what this vision means to you personally. Whatever you are struggling with, write it down. Next to it, write, "Jesus threw _____ into the pit of hell." Then, thank Jesus for what He did for you.

_____

_____

_____

_____

_____

_____

_____

_____

_____

_____

_____

_____

_____

_____

_____

_____

_____

_____

_____

_____

_____

_____

_____

_____

_____

~Day 93~

SEE THE WORLD THROUGH MY NAIL-PIERCED HANDS

I had a vision. In the vision, I was in Heaven, and Jesus said, "I want to show you something." He put my hands in front of my eyes and said, "What do you see?" I said, "Jesus, I don't see anything. I see darkness. I cannot see anything beyond the darkness." He then showed me a vision of the men pounding nails in His hands as He was in excruciating pain, enduring the crucifixion. He then lifted His hands in front of My eyes and said, "What do you see now?" His hands were pointed towards the earth. I could see through the holes in His nail-pierced hands. I saw light. I saw miraculous healings take place. I saw His people destroying darkness wherever they went. They were not afraid of the darkness, rather they had a revelation that they were the light of the world. They were bringing Heaven to earth. I saw hopeless situations turn into miracles. He said these words:

"This is what happens when My people see the world through the cross. I long for My people to understand that the cross changed everything. Without the cross, there is no hope. When I rose from the dead, supernatural power made the impossible possible because I live in you. When you get the revelation that the impossible is possible, that is when the cross makes a difference in your life and you start destroying darkness as I did when I walked the earth. When you understand the power and the love of the cross, you can't help but share it with others. My everlasting love for My people makes the impossible possible. My love through you destroys darkness on the earth.

"Child, do you desire more boldness to share the good news of the gospel with the lost? I will surely give it to you. Ask Me for it. When you understand that it is I Who is working through you, you will have no reason to fear. I long to see the captives set free. That is why I came. I love the captives, and I want to see them set free with My love. Share the love and power of the cross with the lost so they will be forever in My Kingdom. My heart burns for them.

"Child, let Me love on you today in a special way. Come into the secret place. Let Me transform you so that, wherever you spend the rest of the day, people will be transformed by your light, your joy, and My love through you."

Luke 23:33; Luke 1:37; 1 John 3:8; Matthew 5:14; 6:10; Isaiah 61; John 14:12

Prayer: Jesus, thank You for reminding me that the cross changed everything. Help me to continue to see the world through Your nail-pierced hands and resurrection. Please give me a boldness to share the power and love of the cross with the lost. In Your name, Amen.

Day 93 ~ See The World Through My Nail-Pierced Hands

*Spend some time today looking at your world through Jesus' nail-pierced hands. Even place yourself in the vision and look at an impossible situation. Picture that impossible situation in your mind. Next, picture yourself looking through Jesus' nail-pierced hands. Picture this impossible situation being possible because of the cross and resurrection. Keep looking through Jesus' nail-pierced hands until you get a revelation that the impossible is possible in your life. Start proclaiming and decreeing that your Daddy is the God of the impossible. Renew your mind to believe the impossible. Picture yourself bringing Heaven to earth wherever He leads you today.

Journal anything that is on your heart.

~Day 94~

CHILD, TAKE YOUR PEACE BACK!

"Precious one, I see how the enemy tells you all the reasons why you shouldn't trust Me. Beloved, I tell you again that I am for you, not against you. My Word tells you all the reasons why you can trust Me. Renew your mind with the truth that I am always on your side no matter what.

"Child, I was beaten so that you could have everlasting peace. I want you to take your peace back from the enemy. Don't give him a foothold in your life. He is the father of lies. You can trust Me, precious child.

"Beloved, the peace I give you does not come from the world. It comes from Me. I am your perfect peace. You will only find true peace through Me, and we are one. Remember, we became one at the cross. We are one! Peace lives in you now. Take it, child, it is your precious inheritance. Let it break out!

"Precious one, I want you to have a foundation of trust. I want you to trust that I am good. I love to bless you. I love it when you are filled with peace from trusting that your Daddy is good.

"Child, do you need a breakthrough in the area of trusting Me? It's ok, precious one, to admit that you don't always trust Me. I want to heal you of this and show you My loving kindness. Come, stay in My embrace and let Me show you that you can trust Me. Come in Daddy's arms right now and take your peace back. Your Daddy is waiting. I love you, My beloved!

"When it looks like things are falling apart in your life or in certain situations, I want you to renew your mind and say out loud, 'I will trust My Daddy. He wants the best for me and things are happening in the spiritual realm right now. I can always trust My Daddy! He is good all the time!' Child, let this be an opportunity to grow and go higher, the desire of your heart."

Romans 8:31; 12:2; Isaiah 53:5; 9:6; John 14:27; Proverbs 3:5

Prayer:

Jesus, I take back the peace You gave me at the cross in Your name. I choose to trust You. You are so good to me all the time. I cannot find true peace in anything the world offers. Show me that true peace comes from You alone and I receive it now in Your precious name, Amen.

*Spend some time writing Jesus a letter thanking Him
for being beaten so you could have peace.*

~Day 95~

YOUR PRAYERS ARE POWERFUL!

"Child, do you really realize that I hear every single one of your prayers? Do you fully understand that, when you pray, I hear every single word you say? Do you know that I am as much there with you as if you were talking to someone in front of you? I am not far off in the distance somewhere. I am with you at all times. I live in you. You can't get any more real or closer than that. I hear you.

"Precious one, I hear your prayers, every single one. They are very, very powerful. When you pray, I release angels on your behalf and on the behalf of others you pray for. Many things happen in the spiritual realm that you may not even know about or see, but I promise you that things are indeed happening the moment you start praying.

"I love it when you pray with authority. I want to give you a deeper revelation of the authority My Son purchased for you. When you know your authority, your prayers are filled with faith. Oh, how it pleases Me when I hear your faith and trust in Me.

"Beloved, never cease praying and believing that I am good and I hear every single one of your petitions and am moving on your behalf. You will see the full results of all of your prayers in Heaven. You have touched more situations and people than you will ever know. Child, keep praying! I hear you!"

Hebrews 11:6; 1 Thessalonians 5:17; Philippians 4:6; Psalm 116:1-2

Prayer:

Heavenly Daddy, I thank You so much that You never ignore me and You are never distracted when I pray to You. Thank You for the reminder that You hear every single one of My prayers, and, even though it seems like nothing is happening, I thank You that You are always moving on my behalf. I desire a deeper revelation of My authority so that I can pray with boldness, and I thank You for answering this cry of my heart. I love fellowshipping with You. In Jesus' name, Amen.

*Today, keep renewing your mind with, "My Daddy hears every single one of my prayers. He hears me every time I cry out to Him, and He is moving Heaven and earth on my behalf." Thank Him for hearing you today.

Spend some time journaling all of the answered prayers that you can remember. Spend some time praising and thanking your Heavenly Daddy that He hears you and is so faithful.

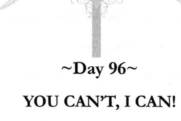

~Day 96~

YOU CAN'T, I CAN!

"Child, I've seen you struggle. I've seen you striving in your own strength. I've seen you trying to solve your problems on your own. I've seen you give up, and I've seen you fail.

"Precious child of Mine, I want you to know that you cannot truly succeed in your own strength. When you give up trying and say, 'Daddy, I can't do it, but you can,' that is when you will see true breakthrough happening in your life. You can do all things through My Son Who strengthens you. However, I want you to learn that you cannot have true breakthrough in your own strength and striving.

"Beloved, give Me all your struggles. Give them all to Me. Let Me show you how to be more than a conqueror when you let My Son live through you and give you the strength to stop all striving.

"Dear child, you can't do it, but I can. When you realize this, you will be transformed in every area of your life. Once you get a powerful revelation that your old man died on the cross with Jesus, you will be transformed. You died and were resurrected with Jesus. He lives in you. Let My Son's life in you cause you to rise above every trial and struggle that comes your way. Let Him do it effortlessly through you. You cannot do it in your own effort. However, you can do all things through My Son who strengthens you. I say in My Word that all things are possible to those who believe. Child, do you really believe My Son lives in you? Let Me give you this powerful, life-changing revelation.

"Beloved, give it to Me. The thing that you have been holding on to, give it to Me. I can do it for you. My desire is to take care of you. There is nothing I cannot do for you. Precious child of Mine, will you let Me help you? Will you stop trying to do it on your own?"

Philippians 4:13; Romans 8:37; Romans 6:3-9; Colossians 1:27; Mark 9:23

Prayer:

Daddy, I can't, but You can. Come and take over! Give me the revelation that Christ lives in me, and He can do it; I can't. I surrender all to You right now. In Jesus' name, Amen.

*Spend some time thinking about some things that you desire to give over to Daddy that you know you have been trying to do in your own strength. Surrender it all to Him.

Make a list of things that you want to fully surrender to your Heavenly Daddy. Write out, "Heavenly Daddy, I give _____ to You today. I can't, but You can."

_____

_____

_____

_____

_____

_____

_____

_____

_____

_____

_____

_____

_____

_____

_____

_____

_____

_____

_____

_____

_____

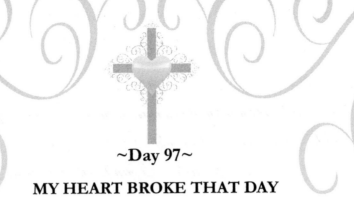

~Day 97~

MY HEART BROKE THAT DAY

My son had surgery and the wound he was dealing with was red and swollen. He was in excruciating pain no matter how much prescribed pain medication we gave him. It was heartbreaking for me to watch him go through the pain, and I wanted to take it from him. As I had tears in my eyes, the Lord spoke to me and reminded me about how He felt when Jesus endured the cross and the cup of wrath. He gave me the following vision.

I saw Jesus' body ripped to shreds from His beating. I saw skin hanging and I saw Him filled with open wounds all over His body. He had nothing to numb the pain. He was in excruciating pain and was red, swollen, and bleeding all over. I saw when He willingly put the cross on top of the open wounds on His shoulders. I saw Jesus cry out in pain. Next, I saw a vision of the Father's heart torn in two just like the veil was torn in two the moment Jesus gave up His Spirit. Next, I heard the Father say:

"It broke My heart to see My Son in so much pain. It broke My heart. I am a loving God. I love My Son. It pained Me to no end to see what He endured in order to set My children free. It pained Me. I wanted to take Him in My arms and love on Him and comfort Him. My heart ached that day. Beloved, My love for you prevented Me from taking that cup from My Son. Please know, precious one, that it was love that came down to save you. It was love that endured the cross. It was love that kept My Son on the cross. It was pure love that endured your cup of wrath. This was all done in love for you, My precious child. Even though it was very painful to watch My Son be crushed, We (Father, Son, and Holy Spirit) were all filled with joy knowing what His beating, death, and resurrection meant for you. We had joy unspeakable thinking about the freedom you would be experiencing. We had joy unspeakable thinking about spending eternity with you.

"Child, don't think it is any different for Me when I see you suffer in any way. It saddens Me to see you in pain. It grieves Me to see you in emotional or physical pain. Child, I want you to know what Jesus went through for you. I want you to see what He purchased in order to set you free. If you are suffering in any way, give it all to Me and let Me comfort you."

Isaiah 53:5; Galatians 5:1; 1 Peter 5:7; Psalm 55:22; Isaiah 53:10

Prayer:

Daddy, thank You for reminding me how You care about me when I am in pain. I am going to give You all of my burdens today. Let My heart break for the pain and suffering Jesus went through for me. Let me see His love as He endured my cup of wrath and transform me. In His name, Amen.

*Meditate on Daddy's heart of love as He watched His Son suffer on our behalf. Ask to feel Daddy's arms of love wrapped around you in a special way. Give any pain you are carrying to Him. Give all your burdens to Him until you feel His peace. Spend some time praising Jesus for enduring your cup of wrath.

Journal what this vision and these words personally mean to you.

~Day 98~

OVERFLOWING JOY

"My child, come into My presence. Come spend time with Your Daddy. I will even make you laugh. I love to have fun with My children. I am filled with joy in your presence. It brings Me much joy to have fellowship with you.

"Come, let Me fill you with My joy. I was filled with joy when I thought of you before the foundations of the world. I was filled with joy at the thought of sending My Son to die for you so that you could have a rich inheritance right now and an abundant life filled with unspeakable joy.

"If you are lacking joy, come into My presence. Come into the secret place, and I will fill you to the overflow with my unending joy. Come, let's have fun! Come, let's laugh together. Being with you brings Me joy.

"There is no condemnation in My presence, only joy. There is no anger in My presence, only joy. There is no guilt or shame in My presence, only joy. My Son took all that for you on the cross so that you could be filled with My joy. Come, be filled."

Psalm 16:11; Ephesians 1:4

Prayer:

Father, let me get to know Your joy, Your laughter, Your sense of humor in my daily life. I pray that as I go into the secret place, You would reveal Your joy to me and fill me to the overflow with it. Help me to experience the fullness of Your joy in my daily life and even in my struggles. Help me to proclaim to others that You are a God of joy, laughter, and fun and that You are in a good mood. Daddy, I thank You for Your joy. In Jesus' name, Amen.

*Spend some time telling Daddy that you need to feel the joy of His presence today in a special way. Ask Him to make you laugh by either showing you something or saying something to you. He loves it when you laugh with Him. Have fun with Him.

Meditate on Psalm 16:11. What does this verse mean to you?

Ask Holy Spirit to give you a deeper revelation of Psalm 16:11
and write down what He shares with you and be blessed.

_____

_____

_____

_____

_____

_____

_____

_____

_____

_____

_____

_____

_____

_____

_____

_____

_____

~Day 99~

THE TABLES HAVE BEEN TURNED

I saw a vision of Jesus. I saw Him as He was carrying the cross and having difficulty walking to Calvary. I saw crowds of people on the side of the road mocking Him. I saw them yelling insults at Jesus because He was about to die a criminal's death. I could see the demons through these peoples' eyes as they were yelling and screaming evil things at Jesus. Jesus was in excruciating pain from His beating and wounds. However, He looked at them with eyes of love focused on His love mission for us. Next, I heard these words:

"My precious child, I was mocked that day. I became a public spectacle. The enemy thought that He actually had a chance, but I bought you back with My precious blood. I was mocked for you so that you can mock him anytime he tries to come at you with his schemes and plans. He is nothing. I made a public spectacle of the enemy by triumphing over him at the cross. I have given you all power and authority over the entire kingdom of darkness. Let this truth sink in. Whenever the demonic realm tries to put symptoms of sickness in your body, remember that I have given you all power and authority over it. Just laugh, child. Just laugh. Remind the enemy that he is defeated and was humiliated that day. Laugh at him! Let's laugh at him together. He is nothing. Laugh at him. Do not fear him. You belong to Me. Show him your joy in Me, and then forget about him and focus on Me and My truth. The truth is that you are My child and I have you under My wings of protection. Renew your mind with this precious truth. Focus on the fact that you are more than a conqueror in Me. He Who is in you is much greater than he who is in the world. You are filled with Me, you are filled with My Kingdom, you are filled with My love, and you are filled with My glory. You are supernatural because the King lives in you. There is nothing that is impossible for those who believe, nothing! Let the truth sink in that you belong to the greatest Kingdom that will ever exist. The tables have been turned. I have made you more than victorious because of My great love for you."

Colossians 2:15; 1:27; Luke 10:19; Psalm 91; 1 John 4:4; Romans 8:37

Prayer:

Jesus, thank You so much for all that You purchased for me because of Your great love for me. Thank You for reminding me that You have given me everything I need to rid the enemy of any power in my life. I am more than a conqueror because I am in You and You are in me. I give You all glory and praise, precious Jesus. In Your name, Amen.

Journal about what this vision personally means to you.

_____

_____

_____

_____

_____

_____

_____

_____

_____

_____

_____

_____

_____

_____

_____

_____

_____

_____

_____

_____

_____

_____

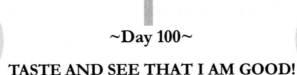

~Day 100~

TASTE AND SEE THAT I AM GOOD!

I saw a vision of a huge banquet table. It was so long that I could not see the end of it. It was full of different kinds of food on it. Jesus was at the table and I heard Him tell people on the streets outside, "Come and see what I prepared for you." I saw a huge crowd of people come to the table. They sat at the table, took a little bit of food, but didn't eat it. Some of them thought it smelled weird. Some of them picked up some food on their forks and played around with it, but decided to put it down. All of the people left without actually tasting the food. I saw them leave and tell other people on the street, "The food smells different. It looks weird. Don't go in there. It's a waste of time." However, a small group of people went in anyway. They were hungry for something different. They sat at the table. They not only smelled the food, but they actually tasted the food and ate it. When they tasted the food, their eyes opened wide with delight. They not only tasted the food, they took more and more on their plates. They knew for themselves that the food was delicious because they experienced it for themselves. They ignored all the lies that others told them about the food. When Jesus saw the joy on their faces and that these hungry people were enjoying the feast that He had prepared for them, He was very touched and started weeping.

Next, Jesus said, "I want you to taste and see that I am good. I want you to truly experience Me. Some people will tell you lies about Me and about things of the Spirit because they have not tasted and experienced Me. They will tell you that I am only to be learned about and not experienced. I adore My children who are hungry for more. I delight in the ones who truly want to experience everything that is theirs, everything I purchased for them. It brings Me great joy to have intimate relationship with My intimate ones. I love to touch these children in a special way, however I am hungry to touch all of My children. I long for them all to experience Me, to taste and see that I am good. You cannot truly get to know Me without experiencing Me. Come, let Me show you who I really am. Come, get to know Me intimately. Come, experience Me in a whole new way. Come, taste and see that I am good. Come and see that I am the only food that satisfies. No other food can satisfy you like I can. I am the Bread Of Life. Come to Me and you will never hunger again. Come and taste My love and goodness. I am waiting for you, My beloved."

Psalm 34:8; Matthew 4:4; John 6:35; Isaiah 55:1-2; 1 Peter 2:3; Matthew 22

*Spend some time experiencing Jesus in a whole new way today. Pray in the Spirit and experience your lover with you.

Write a letter to Jesus, the lover of your soul, telling Him you accept
the invitation to come truly experience Him in a new way.
Share what is on your heart with Him.

_____
_____
_____
_____
_____
_____
_____
_____
_____
_____
_____
_____
_____
_____
_____
_____
_____
_____
_____
_____
_____

~Day 101~

DO YOU REALIZE THAT YOUR DAD IS THE KING OF KINGS?

"My precious child, good things come to those who realize that I am their Dad. I am the King of Kings. I created the universe and everything in it with My life-giving words. You belong to My Kingdom now! Whatever I have is yours. What do you need? Are you lacking in any area of your life? I want you to get a revelation that your Dad is the King of Kings. There is nothing that I wouldn't do for you!

"Beloved, see yourself with a crown on your head and a scepter in your hand. See Me putting a ring on your finger. Start proclaiming and decreeing what you need from My Kingdom and watch it manifest on the earth. Start decreeing victory over your problems and watch your circumstances change.

"You are royalty! There is no greater Kingdom to belong to than Mine. The kingdom of darkness is miniscule compared to My Kingdom. Don't let that pathetic kingdom deceive you into thinking that you have no power. I tell you that the power of life or death is in your tongue. Your words, as royal children, have power to change the world. Start proclaiming and decreeing words of power in your life and in your circumstances. Continue to stand against all lies from the enemy. Speak life-giving words of power, not curses. For I tell you again, you belong to My Kingdom and you have royal authority."

Genesis 1; Isaiah 61:10; Proverbs 18:21; Ephesians 6:11; Job 22:28

Prayer:

Heavenly Daddy, I pray that You would help me to see that I am important in Your Kingdom. I am a royal child with a destiny. I pray that You would help me to see any curses I am speaking over my life and help me to replace them with Your life-giving words. Thank You for reminding me that I have the power to decree a thing and it shall be done. Help me to bring Your Kingdom to earth. Continue to show me that I have nothing to fear because my Dad is the King of Kings! In Jesus' name, Amen.

*Keep reminding yourself throughout the day, "My Dad is the King of Kings. I am royalty. I am from another Kingdom, and all things are possible to them that believe." Make some victorious decrees today.

Make a list of all of the blessings you can think of as a result of
your Dad being the "King of Kings."

~Day 102~

I REMOVED THE VEIL THAT WAS BETWEEN US

I saw a vision of a woman wearing a veil as if on her wedding day. It was a beautiful white veil, and it was covering her face. Suddenly, in the Spirit, I saw a vision of the veil in the temple being torn in two when Jesus gave up His Spirit. After I saw the veil in the temple being torn in two, I immediately saw Jesus in front of the woman wearing the veil, and He lifted the veil off of her face as a husband does on the bride's wedding day. When the veil was removed, the woman was able to gaze into Jesus' eyes of love. Jesus also looked at His bride with eyes of love. He then took the bride in His arms and gently kissed her on the cheek. He said these words:

"You are My precious bride forever. I want to kiss you forever and keep you in My embrace for all eternity. I love you so much and nothing will ever separate you from My love, nothing. My precious bride, I want you to understand that there is no more barrier between us. I removed the veil that was between us. I removed the sin that separated us through My death and resurrection. The moment you accepted Me is the moment I came to be with you forever. That is the moment you became My beautiful, precious bride whom I adore.

"My precious bride, we are one. Let Me be the husband you have been longing for. Let Me love on you the way you were destined to be loved. Let Me show you that when you speak to Me, it melts My heart, and I can't get enough of your presence. I love it when you give your heart to Me. It brings Me unspeakable joy when you trust Me with your whole heart. It overwhelms Me when you tell Me how much you love Me.

"I long for My people to know my love for them. I long for my people to know Me as their faithful husband Who will never, ever break covenant with them. I long for My people to know how I truly see them. I long for My people to understand that My heart aches with love for them in a way that they could never imagine. My heart aches with love for My beautiful bride. I love you infinitely more than words can describe."

Mark 15:37-38; 2 Corinthians 3:18; Romans 8:38-39; Proverbs 3:5-6; Song of Solomon 4:7

Prayer: Jesus, thank You so much for removing the veil of separation between us. I will focus on Your eyes of love today. Help me to surrender my whole heart to You. Help me to see You as my husband Who loves me. Amen.

*Picture yourself as the bride in this vision. Picture Jesus gazing into your eyes and picture His eyes of love looking at you right now. Picture yourself giving Him your whole heart. Tell Him how much you love Him.

Journal about what this vision means to you personally and then thank Jesus for removing the veil.

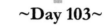

~Day 103~

I AM NOT MAD AT YOU!

"My precious child, I am not mad at you. I do not look down and frown at you in disgust. No, child, when I see you, I smile. When I see you, my heart flutters because of the love I feel for you. When I look at you, I am filled with such joy and extremely passionate love for you.

"Dear one, my precious Son Jesus took all of My wrath on the cross for you. All of My wrath was poured out on My Son the moment all of your sins were placed on Him. He was punished in your place. It was very painful for Me to not be able to look at Him in the moment He cried out, 'My God, My God, why have You forsaken Me?' In that moment, every single sin you have ever committed or will ever commit was placed on Him, and, because of this love act, I remember your sins no more. I am not mad at you. Because Jesus was forsaken at the cross, I will never, ever forsake you, no never!

"My Son took your sins and gave you His righteousness. Because of this trade, when I look at you, I see you as righteous as My Son. Remember when I spoke in an audible voice, 'This is My dearly loved Son, who brings Me great joy'? This is how I see you. I see you as My dearly loved child who brings Me great joy! No, I am not mad at you!

"Beloved, you have been declared innocent because of My Son. You have been set free because of My Son. When I look at you, I see Christ in you, the hope of glory. Child, I rejoice over you with singing. I am not mad at you, rather, I am singing love songs over you. You are precious to Me."

John 1:29; Romans 3:23-26; Hebrews 8:12; Romans 5:17; 1 John 4:10; Zephaniah 3:17

Prayer:

Heavenly Daddy, whenever the enemy comes in to tell me that You are mad at me, remind me that Jesus took all of Your wrath for me on the cross. Thank You that You love me and You rejoice over me with singing. Thank You, Jesus, for giving me Your righteousness. Thank You, Jesus, for taking my punishment. Lord, give me a perfect hatred for all sin so that I can live a holy life that is pleasing to You. In Jesus' name, Amen.

*Tell yourself today, "My Daddy is not mad at me, He is mad about me because of what Jesus did for me."

Journal about how these words from today's devotion have touched your heart. Thank Jesus for taking your cup of wrath.

~Day 104~

TONGUES IS A LOVE GIFT TO YOU

I saw a vision of a woman praying in tongues. As she was praying in the Spirit, I heard Holy Spirit weeping because He was so touched. As the woman continued to pray in tongues, her mind became clear. As she looked around her room, even the paint on the walls seemed brighter to her. She started to feel joy, power, and freedom from mind strongholds. Holy Spirit was telling her what to pray in the Spirit. Holy Spirit knew what she was struggling with and was able to help her pray against it. Next, I saw a vision of angels waiting in Heaven. They were waiting for this woman to pray in the Spirit so that they could be sent to protect her daughter later in the day. I saw a vision of the daughter being protected from a fatal car wreck. The Lord showed me that this woman prayed for this incident without knowing it. Next, I heard these words:

"My precious child, Holy Spirit is My gift to you. Praying in the Spirit is my gift to you. When you let Holy Spirit help you pray, you receive power. You receive revelation and boldness. You receive words of knowledge. You allow the Kingdom of Heaven to work on your behalf. You receive what you need to walk into your destiny. You receive encouragement. You receive deliverance. You receive peace. You receive all that you need. Holy Spirit knows exactly what you need when you need it, and He loves to help you. We (Father, Son, and Holy Spirit) are filled with so much joy when you understand the fullness of the gift of tongues. Beloved, continue to pray in the Spirit, and you will see major changes in your life and in the lives of those you have been praying for. When you pray in the Spirit, your mind will be clearer because it will be at complete rest. You have been given this love gift because you are so loved by your Heavenly Daddy. Every gift is given to you out of love. Go into the secret place and let Holy Spirit help you pray for everything you need and receive true rest that is your inheritance."

Psalm 103:20; Acts 1:8; Mark 16:15-18; Acts 19:6; 1 Corinthians 14:1-5; Jude 20; Isaiah 28:11; Ephesians 1:18; 6:18; Romans 8:26-27; Isaiah 28:11-12; 63:14

Prayer: Heavenly Daddy, thank You for the gift of tongues. I pray that You would put a desire in me to pray in the Sprit whenever I can. Thank You for helping me in more ways than I even know by letting Holy Spirit pray for me and giving my mind complete rest. I love You, Daddy. In Jesus' precious name, Amen.

*Spend some time praying in the Spirit and thanking Daddy for this wonderful gift.

** See page 269 for Baptism in the Holy Spirit prayer

*After spending time praying in tongues, write down what you
experienced and what Holy Spirit shared with you.
Thank Holy Spirit for knowing exactly what you need to pray for.*

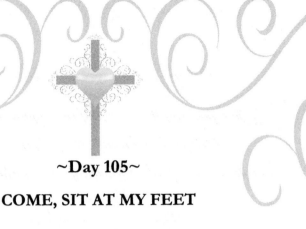

~Day 105~

COME, SIT AT MY FEET

"My child, My precious child, I love it when you sit at My feet like Mary. Mary chose what is good, what is helpful, what is healing—to listen, to receive My life giving words.

"When you sit at My feet, you are in a place of rest. When you are resting, you are better able to hear My voice whispering to you how much I love you. My Holy Spirit is constantly reminding you of My unfailing, everlasting love. However, it is in the place of rest that you are able to receive and hear Holy Spirit's reminders of My love. Child, nothing can separate you from My love, absolutely nothing!

"Come, sit at My feet, stay in My presence, and you will receive everything that you need to get you through any trial that comes your way. Come, sit at My feet and let Me remind you that My Son already purchased your victory when He rose from the dead. Come, sit at My feet and let Me remind you that My Son purchased all of your inheritance. He has given you every spiritual blessing.

"Come, sit at My feet and receive all that I have for you. Let Me pour out My unending love on you. Come, sit at My feet and let Me love on you. Come, sit at My feet, and you will feel My peace that only I can give you.

"Child, I am waiting, and I am eager to spend time with you. Come, sit at My feet, and you will never be the same."

Luke 10:38-42; Romans 8:38; Ephesians 1:3

Prayer:

Jesus, I am choosing like Mary to go sit at Your feet today. Please give me the rest I am searching for, the rest that only You can give me when I am sitting in Your presence at Your feet. I long for a deep revelation of my inheritance. Thank You for Your love for me. Help me to hear the Holy Spirit's love whispers to me all day long. In Jesus' precious name, Amen.

*Ask Holy Spirit to speak some love whispers to you and spend some time writing them down on a sheet of paper. Keep this paper with you throughout the day to remind yourself how much you are loved by the King.

What does it mean to you to be sitting at Jesus' feet?

~Day 106~

I AM RUNNING AFTER YOU WITH OPEN ARMS

"My child, why do you run away from Me? Why do you feel shame? I did not create shame. It came in at the Garden of Eden when My children were deceived by the evil one.

"Child, the more you run away, the more I continue to pursue you. I will not stop running after you until I catch you, My bride. I am the Good Shepherd, and I always bring My sheep back to the fold in the protection of My loving arms. I will do the same for you."

After hearing those words, I saw a vision of a woman running very fast. She had fear and shame on her face. Jesus was running after the woman. The woman was trying to run away from Him. She was thinking, "Oh no! I can't let Him see me until I can stop sinning. I am full of shame at what I've done. I can't bear to face Him." Jesus kept running faster until He reached His daughter's arm, and He proceeded to pull her tightly into His arms of love. He was holding the woman tightly in His arms. He was saying to her, "You are My precious bride. I love you. Come back to Me. Stay with Me. Let Me show you how much I love you." As He was saying these things, He was gazing deeply into her eyes and caressing her hair. His bride started to melt in His arms of unconditional love. She had finally found the peace, joy, and love she was searching for, and she surrendered herself to His love. She was transformed in His arms.

John 10:11; Luke 15:20

Prayer:

Jesus, thank You for always pursuing me with Your love even in my failures. Thank You that Your love never changes. Jesus, help me to stop running away so that I can melt in Your arms and receive the love that You have for me. When the enemy condemns me, show me this loving picture of how You love me and will never let me go. Remind me that I will always be Your bride. Remind me that shame disappears in the arms of My loving husband. In Your name, Amen.

*Spend some time telling Jesus that you are sorry for the times that you ran away from Him to hide. Tell Him that you don't want to hide anymore. Spend some time melting in His arms of love.

Write a letter to Jesus thanking Him for always continuing to pursue you with His love.

~Day 107~

I LOVE UNITY

I saw a vision of the body of believers holding hands in a big circle around the earth walking towards the center of the earth. Next, I saw demons come in and whisper things in some of the people's ears. When these children opened the door to the enemy's thoughts and lies, I saw these demons take their arms and crash them down on the people's arms, until some of them were no longer holding hands. There was disunity and confusion among the body, and they stopped walking together.

Next, I saw a vision of this same body of believers holding hands. They were again in a huge circle around the earth. Their grips were very tight. When the enemy came in, they didn't listen and continued to walk. They were standing against the enemy. They all continued to walk in unity towards the center of the earth. Finally, I saw them all reach the middle. Right in the middle of the earth, there was a huge pit that was very deep. I saw that, as the believers were walking towards the center in unity, the works of the devil would fall into the pit. I saw words like disunity, sickness, lying, bitterness, un-forgiveness, jealousy, and every evil work go down into the pit. The believers were left standing together in unity in victory. When they had reached the center, they started praising Jesus together. It was the most beautiful worship I have ever heard. Love prevailed as the believers stayed in unity, and darkness stayed in the pit. I heard Jesus say this:

"Unity is the desire of My heart for My body. Imagine what My people would be able to accomplish if they stayed in unity together, destroying the kingdom of darkness and bringing Heaven to earth. Do not let the devil destroy you, your families, or the ministries and friendships I have given you. Disunity is a huge weapon of the kingdom of darkness. It grieves Me when you continue to hold on to un-forgiveness, jealousy, and every evil work of the devil. I tell you that I have given you the power to overcome disunity. Let the powerful love I poured into you through the Holy Spirit give you the power to love and forgive others so that you can be free and walk into your destinies. I love unity. I love it when you all get along. I love it when you all recognize each other's uniqueness. I love it when you cheer people on who

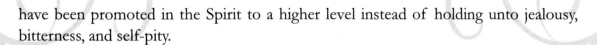

have been promoted in the Spirit to a higher level instead of holding unto jealousy, bitterness, and self-pity.

"Precious one, when you understand the powerful, extreme love I have for you, you will be able to stand against all of the enemy's thoughts, lies, and schemes that want to cause division and disunity. Know that I want you to soak in My love, and then give it out to others and forgive them. I want you to see that when someone wrongs you, they are under the influence of the enemy. See them for who they are, not for how the enemy is manifesting through them. When you see them through My eyes, you will be able to walk in love. I love unity.

"Precious one, I also realize that maybe you have tried to reconcile with someone who was unwilling. You have displayed My heart in doing this. Get rid of any un-forgiveness that came in during this time and pray for that person to receive truth. Pray blessings over that person and then go in peace."

John 14:12; 1 Corinthians 1:10; Philippians 2:2; 2 Corinthians 13:11; Ephesians 4:1-6, 27, 31; 6:10-13; 5:11; Colossians 3:14; Psalm 133:1; Luke 10:19; Acts 20:28

Prayer:

Heavenly Daddy, thank You so much for this reminder that it is always Your desire to have peace and unity in Your body of believers. I am sorry for the times I have believed the enemy and caused strife in any way. I vow to use the power You have given me to overcome disunity. I realize that unity can't be forced on some people, but I will do my part to stay in peace, if at all possible, with everyone because that is Your heart. In Jesus' name, Amen.

What does this vision mean to you personally?

Special Addendum: Spend some time thinking about unity and how important it is to our Daddy. Tell Him how sorry you are for the times that you have held onto bitterness, jealousy, un-forgiveness, etc. If there is someone you need to reconcile with, write down their names and pray that Daddy will help you to do that today.

~Day 108~

I'M RAINING KISSES FROM HEAVEN

"I am raining My love kisses from Heaven. Come, My child, come get drenched in My love. This is not an earthly rain, this is a supernatural, Heavenly rain that only I can give.

"Come, those who are thirsty. Come, those who are feeling tired. Come, those who are feeling dry. In My rain, you will find healing. In My rain, you will find the peace you have been searching for. I want to flood you with My unending love. I want each drop to feel like I have come down from Heaven to kiss My bride.

"Do you hear the rain falling? Listen, go to a quiet place. I will show you the rain. Don't bring an umbrella. Don't resist it. I want you to get soaked with My love kisses. Each drop will transform you from the inside out.

"Come! Let's splash together and have fun in My Heavenly rain!"

Matthew 11:28; John 7:37-38

Prayer:

Heavenly Daddy, as I go into a quiet place, I pray that You would rain that supernatural rain on me. Father, drench me in Your love and transform me as only You can do. Let me feel Your rain kisses from Heaven today in a special way. Soak me, saturate me, and drench me in Your everlasting love. Father, I receive it right now. In Jesus' precious, holy name, Amen.

*Go to a quiet place and imagine Daddy's love kisses coming down from Heaven drenching you with His love. Spend some time receiving His love kisses and then give Him some kisses from your heart. Worship Him and love on Him until you feel His oil of joy pouring down on you.

What do you think Heavenly rain symbolizes?

_____

_____

_____

_____

_____

_____

_____

_____

_____

_____

_____

_____

_____

_____

_____

_____

_____

_____

~Day 109~

PLEASE DON'T LEAVE ME

I received a touching vision about Jesus. In the vision, I saw Him brutally beaten hanging on the cross. I saw how grotesque his face looked. He was very disfigured. I saw Him covered in cuts, bruises, and blood. He was lifeless because He had just given up His Spirit.

Next, I hugged Him and was overwhelmed with grief. I was weeping saying, "What did they do to my Jesus?" I kept repeating these words as I was crying. Suddenly, I turned around and saw Jesus. He was wearing a white robe, and He was radiant with glory. He motioned for me to come over to Him and sit on His lap. He said, "Child, this is good news! Now that I died and rose again, I live in you and am with you forever!" He said, "I will never leave you and please don't leave Me." I could see the sadness in His eyes not wanting me to leave Him because of His love for Me. He was gazing deeply in my eyes with His eyes of pure, passionate love. I knew He meant that He always wants me to remember that He is with me, but if I do not acknowledge His presence it's as if I am ignoring or leaving Him. He was drawing me into deeper intimacy with Him and reminding Me that He loves our relationship with Him. He loves it when we converse with Him and love on Him.

Colossians 1:27; Hebrews 13:5; 1 Corinthians 15:3-4

Prayer:

Heavenly Daddy, thank You so much for sending Jesus to die for me. Thank You that, because He died and rose again, He now lives in me. His glory lives in me. His power lives in me. His love lives in me. His healing power lives in me. Thank You that He alone helps me to live the Christian life. I can do nothing without Him working through me. Please give me a deeper revelation of Christ in me, the hope of glory. In Jesus' name, Amen.

*Picture yourself in this vision. I encourage you to go to a quiet place and ask Holy Spirit to show this to you in a personal way. Spend some time lifting up the name of Jesus.

Spend some time writing to Jesus of how sorry you are for the times you have not acknowledged Him. Tell Him how much you love Him until you feel His joy.

_____

_____

_____

_____

_____

_____

_____

_____

_____

_____

_____

_____

_____

_____

_____

_____

_____

_____

~Day 110~

LET MY LOVE CAST OUT ALL YOUR FEAR OF TRUSTING ME

"Precious one, I know people have wounded you. I see you having a hard time trusting that I am for you in every single situation and trial you face. I see you opening the door to fear and anxiety and 'what ifs.' I also see how you believe you need to make things happen instead of waiting on Me and trusting My timing. Beloved, it grieves Me to see you in such torment. Precious child, surrender it to Me. Give it all to Me, and you will feel My perfect peace. Cast all your burdens on Me. Don't carry them any longer. They are weighing you down. Ask Me to remind you of My love for you so that My perfect love can cast out all your fear. Ask Me.

"Child, you will know when you have let My love cast out fear. You will experience a peace that passes all understanding. You will know that you know that you know it in your heart. Your whole countenance will change.

"Beloved, sometimes things take time. Battle any lies of the enemy that tell you that I have forgotten about you or that I don't hear you. Those are lies! I hear every single word you speak to Me, and I never forget what you say. I will never forget you or reject you. Trust Me, child. Trust My timing. You won't miss it when you trust Me. Keep reminding yourself that I love you and always have your best interests at heart.

"Trust Me, precious child. Give it to Me! I want to take it from you and take away all your fear and anxiety and replace it with My love and peace."

Isaiah 40:31; Philippians 4:7; 1 Peter 5:7; 1 John 4:18

Prayer:

Dear Heavenly Daddy, thank You for continually reminding me that I can trust You. Thank You for reminding me that You hear me every time I talk, pray, or cry out to You. You hear every single word. Right now, in the name of Jesus, I repent and renounce participating with fear, and I tell it to go in the name of Jesus. I tell you, fear, to stop tormenting me and get out, and I close the door on you. The truth is that I have nothing to fear because My Daddy always has my best interests at heart. I choose to trust you, Daddy, and I give it all to You now. In Jesus' name, Amen.

*Spend some time letting Daddy love on you today. Just sit and rest in His precious love for you. Remind yourself throughout the day, "I can trust My Daddy all the time because He has plans to prosper me."

Write a letter to your Heavenly Daddy telling Him all the reasons why you can trust His love.

_____
_____
_____
_____
_____
_____
_____
_____
_____
_____
_____
_____
_____
_____
_____
_____
_____
_____
_____
_____
_____
_____
_____

~Day 111~

I WANT TO BLOW YOU AWAY WITH MY LOVE

In October, 2010, there was a mighty wind that blew into the Chicago area where I live. As I was walking my dogs in this powerful wind one day, the Lord gave me a vision. I saw a vision of a woman in a storm. Imagine what a storm looks like. She was being battered by the wind and the rain, and she was filled with fear. She was struggling and restless in the storm. She was exhausted from fighting to get out of it but feeling powerless to change anything. Next, she cried out to Jesus, and He came and took her out of the storm.

Next, I saw Jesus start blowing with His mouth. It was so powerful. It was a mighty wind. This same woman started blowing around in the wind. She was up in the air, being carried by the wind. She was resting as she was being completely carried and supported in the wind. She actually started laughing from the joy, peace, and rest she was feeling. She kept her eyes on Jesus, and, as she did, she felt His passionate love for her. As she got a revelation of His powerful love, she kept resting and laughing.

I heard Him say, "Beloved, I want to blow you away with My love. Come into My wind. I want to show you a whole new world of rest and what that looks like. When you know the passionate love I have for you, you are able to rest and let Me blow you to new heights with My love. My wind is healing, not destructive."

Next, I saw a vision of the Father's hand come down from Heaven through the clouds. His hand then went back up, and I knew in my spirit what He was doing. He was bringing His hand back up to His mouth. Next, I heard Him kiss His hand, and then I heard Him start blowing this kiss to His children. When He blew, it was like the wind we were experiencing in Chicago. It was a powerful, mighty wind. When the kiss reached His children, they were knocked flat on the ground with His love. They were able to let Him pour His passionate love into them, and they were forever changed. He said, "I want to blow you away with My powerful love for you. You will never be the same again. Do you want it? Do you want My powerful love kiss? Come and get it. Come into the mighty wind and receive your kiss from Me. It will fill you with life and power, and you will be transformed. It is your inheritance. Come, receive Daddy's love kiss for you."

Ephesians 3:18; Song of Solomon 1:2; Hebrews 4:9-11

Day 111 ~ I Want to Blow You Away With My Love

Prayer: Heavenly Daddy, I want to stop striving, working, and fighting. I want to experience the true rest that You have for me. Help me to believe that You are good and that I am created to rest in the love and promises You have for me. Remind me that I can do nothing apart from You, absolutely nothing. Remind me when I need to take my peace back from the enemy who wants to steal the rest You have given me as my inheritance. Daddy, help me to receive the love kisses You have for me right now. I want all the kisses I can get from You because they are healing to my entire body. In Jesus' precious name, Amen.

*Picture resting in Jesus' wind and let Him blow you away with His love for you. Picture the Father blowing you love kisses that knock you down and transform you. Then, blow Him a love kiss from your heart.

Journal what this vision means to you personally.

~Day 112~

DISTRACTIONS TAKE YOU AWAY FROM INTIMACY WITH ME

"Dear child, there are so many distractions that can take you away from intimacy with Me. Not every distraction is bad. However, even good things can become distractions and take you away from spending time with Me.

"Precious one, this doesn't make Me upset with you. I adore you. I want to help you. I see how the more distracted you become, the more the enemy steals your peace. I know the desire of your heart is peace and intimacy with Me, and that is why I want to gently show you some things in your life that are robbing you of experiencing deep intimacy with Me.

"Beloved, the enemy constantly tries to take you away from spending time soaking in My presence. He knows that the more time you spend with your Heavenly Daddy, the more joy, peace, and glory you will experience. He knows how you feel refreshed and filled when you spend time with Me. Beloved, some of these distractions are an escape. They prevent you from feeling some emotions that come to the surface, and they keep walls up. I want to do a deep inner healing in your life. Let go of anything that prevents you from experiencing genuine intimacy with Me. I promise you that this journey of going lower will actually take you higher than you've ever been. It will take you into your destiny.

"Let Me heal any fear of intimacy the enemy is attacking you with. I will not hurt you or disappoint you. I want to love on you. That is what you were created for."

1 Corinthians 7:35; Colossians 3:2

Prayer:

Dear Heavenly Daddy, I pray that You would show me what is taking me away from genuine, quality, intimate fellowship with You. I want all that You have for Me and know that the way to receive it is to spend time letting You love on me. Father, help me to give up the distractions that take me away from spending time with You. I desire a closer relationship with You. I want to know You in a deeper, more intimate way. In Jesus' name, Amen.

*Go to a quiet place where there are no distractions. Spend some time being intimate with your Heavenly Daddy. Meditate on how good He is. Meditate on His love for you. When your mind starts to wander or be distracted, just refocus your attention on your Heavenly Daddy. After meditating, start praising Him for His goodness.

Journal how you felt when you went to a quiet place. Were you distracted? Why do you think you were distracted? Write about how you know that you can have victory over distractions in your life. Tell Daddy you want to know Him more intimately. Ask Him what your distractions are.

~Day 113~

IT PAINS ME TO SEE MY CHILDREN SUFFER

I saw a vision of Jesus in a hospital. He was going from room to room weeping as he saw how the patients were suffering. His heart ached, and He took every single one of them in His arms and cradled them.

I then saw a vision of a woman who had just lost her husband at an early age. She was weeping, and I saw Jesus putting His arms around her although she didn't feel His presence, and He was weeping with her.

I then saw a vision of a man at work. He was being treated harshly by his boss. The man was suffering emotionally from the unwarranted abuse. I saw Jesus weeping as He came to comfort the man in His loving arms. Then He said this:

"My precious children, My heart aches to see you suffer with sickness, tragedy, abuse, and anything else that causes you pain. I even hate to see you suffer when it is something that you have done yourself to cause the pain. It pains Me to see My children suffering. I have so much compassion for those who are struggling with pain and sickness. I have cried many, many tears for these precious children of Mine, especially when they believe the lie that I am causing bad things to happen to them.

"Don't let anyone ever tell you that I enjoy to see you suffer. I suffered for you at Calvary. Yes, you will have trials in this life, but I do not enjoy to see you suffer through them. Yes, the trials make you stronger and help you develop perseverance and character, yet it still pains Me to see you suffer in the process.

"I want you to understand My heart of love towards you. I understand suffering. I understand extreme emotional suffering and pain. I understand the hurt of being rejected by loved ones. I understand suffering because I went through it for you, precious one. I understand what you are going through. Child, don't be afraid to tell Me how you are feeling. Don't be afraid to cry out to Me in pain. I want you to cry out to Me so that you can feel Me comforting you. Come to Me when you are experiencing trials and let Me give you the revelation that I have won the victory for you because of My extreme love for you. You are an overcomer."

John 16:33; James 1:2; Hebrews 2:16-18; Jeremiah 33:3

Day 113 ~ It Pains Me to See My Children Suffer

Prayer: Heavenly Daddy, help me to run to You when I am in pain or suffering. Let me feel Your loving arms around me. Thank You for reminding me that You want to comfort me when I am suffering. You are the God of all comfort. Thank You for being my precious Heavenly Father. In Jesus' name, Amen.

*Spend some time crying out to Jesus about any trials, sickness, or struggles you are going through and let Him comfort you and show you the way to victory. Thank Him for overcoming the world for you.

Write a letter to your Heavenly Daddy thanking Him for His comfort. Thank Him for His love and compassion when you experience trials of any kind. Write from your heart and be vulnerable with your precious Heavenly Father.

~Day 114~

I CHOOSE THE REJECTED ONES

I saw a vision. I saw an elementary gym class. I saw the teacher pick two captains who had to pick teams to play games. All of the kids lined up. The two captains were choosing the "best" kids for the teams. There was a little boy there. This boy was small and not very athletic. He was picked on all the time. He was usually rejected by the kids at the school and was always the last one picked for everything. He was sad because he was the last one picked again. He felt so much pain at never feeling wanted or accepted, always rejected.

Next, I saw another vision. I saw two captains, only this time, Jesus was one of the captains. Immediately, Jesus' first pick was the rejected boy. The boy had a huge smile on his face as he realized that Jesus wanted him, and not only that, Jesus picked him first. He experienced the love of Christ, and his whole countenance changed. He was beaming and, for once, felt very special. Next, I heard these words:

"I have a special place in my heart for rejected, broken people. I have such a special place in My heart for them, and I draw near to them. I absolutely love to love on My rejected children in a special way. I love to set them free with My love. I want to give all of My children a revelation that they will never, ever be rejected by Me. I see how these wounded ones are treated, and it grieves My heart. If you have felt wounded and rejected, come to Me. Come and be with Me. Let Me show you that you have a very special place in My heart and in My Kingdom. Let Me show you who you are in Me. Let Me change your countenance. Let Me take away all inferiority. You are not inferior in My eyes, and you never will be. Child, you are absolutely righteous in My eyes because of the blood.

"Beloved, let Me show you how much you mean to Me. Let Me show you My loving kindness. Let Me show you that you are on my team, and I have chosen you to be with Me forever. I love you. Do you hear Me? I love you. Please accept these words for your heart. You are My beloved."

Psalm 34:18; Isaiah 61:1; Romans 5:17

Prayer: Jesus, thank You so much for letting Your love heal all of my rejection wounds. Thank You for reminding me that You are ever so close to me when I am in pain. Jesus, show me who I am in You and how You see me. As I go into the secret place, I long for You to share with Me how You feel about the brokenhearted so I can share this love with them. In Your name, Amen.

Day 114 ~ I Choose The Rejected Ones

Do you feel inferior? Have you suffered a lot of rejection? Write a letter to Daddy telling Him that you want all of that out of your life. Write down how that has effected you. Next, write down truth-filled verses about who you are in Christ. The truth is that you are not inferior. You have a special destiny in the Kingdom of God.

~Day 115~

YOU ARE CLOTHED WITH ME

I saw a vision of Jesus after He was scourged. He had wounds all over Him. His clothes became glued to His body from the dried blood. Next, I saw men rolling the dice for His clothing. I saw the winner jump up in excitement. He was excited that he would be causing Jesus excruciating pain in the process of removing His clothes. I saw the winner rip Jesus' clothes off. Jesus was in agony as the clothes were stuck to the dried blood. When the clothes were finally ripped off of Jesus, I saw a vision of the old man being ripped off of His people. The old man was instantly ripped off of His people. Then, I saw Christians putting Christ on like clothing. I heard these words:

"The moment you accepted Me, you became a new creation. You clothed yourself with Me. The moment you accepted Me, the old man died and was removed. I made you alive in Me. The moment you accepted Me, the impossible became possible, and the natural became supernatural because I translated you into My Kingdom. You are a new creation. You can no longer go back to the old. Let it sink in that you are a new creation, and that's what I see.

"We are one. We are united. Before the foundation of the world, I knew I had a mission for us to become one. I love you so much, precious child of Mine. You belong to Me. Picture yourself clothed with Me right now. Picture yourself enveloped in My protection as I cover you with Myself. You are so precious to Me. Picture yourself clothed in My righteousness because you are. I came to set you free and make you a new creation. I came to give you a better life. I did this because of My everlasting, unending, undying love for you. I came to make you one with Me, My beloved. I love being one with you, precious child. It brings Me great joy. Let this truth sink in."

Mark 15:24; 2 Corinthians 5:17; 1 Corinthians 15:22; Colossians 1:13; 2:11; 1 Corinthians 2:16; Galatians 3:27

Prayer:

Jesus, thank You so much for making me a new creation. Help me hunger for a deeper revelation of what it means to be clothed with You and Your righteousness. I pray that You would give me words and pictures to help me understand this in a deeper way. Thank You for coming to set me free and give me a life that is greater than my wildest dreams. In Your name, Amen

Spend some time thanking Jesus for enduring tremendous suffering at the cross so that you could be free. Thank Him for making you a new creation. Write about what this vision personally means to you. Do you feel like a new creation? Why or why not?

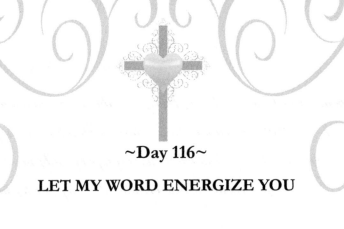

~Day 116~

LET MY WORD ENERGIZE YOU

I saw a vision of a man lacking energy, feeling down and tired. Next, I saw him drinking an energy drink. He started feeling some energy from the drink, but it only lasted a certain amount of time. Next, I saw him drinking another energy drink in order to feel energy again. It was a continuous cycle of trying to feel better (emotionally and physically) and trying to feel more energy to make it through the day.

Next, I saw Jesus. The next time that the man felt tired and lacking energy, Jesus gave him the Word. Jesus showed him some things in the Word. Immediately, the man felt life and power in his body. I saw the words from the pages going into this man's body. He felt supernatural peace of mind, energy, and power that he had never experienced in his life. As he went throughout the day, as he was beginning to be attacked with fatigue, depression, etc., I saw the man pick up the Word and immediately he would start to feel full of life. He would start to feel his whole body change. He would feel joy, and he was filled again.

Jesus said, "Beloved, when you feel down or tired, fill yourself with the Word. Drink and soak up the Word. I am the Word, and I am life. Fill yourself with the precious truths of the Word. Read about My love for you. Read about what I did, how I see you. Read about Me giving you My righteousness. Read about how I acquitted you from your sins. Read about how I no longer condemn you. Let all these truths fill you with life and power. When you continue to stay in My Word, which is My gift to you, you will continue to feel life. You will continue to feel joy. You will continue to renew your mind and get rid of those depressing thoughts from the enemy that bring you down. Precious one, let My Word fill you and bring you supernatural energy and an alertness of mind that surpasses all understanding. My peace of mind, supernatural energy, and power is not as the world gives, it is much greater than you could ever imagine."

Hebrews 4:12 AMP - "For the Word that God speaks is alive and full of power {making it active, operative, energizing, and effective}"; John 1:1; 6:63; Romans 5:17; Romans 12:2; John 14:27; Romans 4:7

Prayer: Jesus, thank You for reminding me to continually fill myself with Your Word. Your Word is life, peace, and even supernatural energy to me to help me get through the day. Thank You for the gift of the Word. You are the Word. Whenever I start to get attacked by the enemy, let Your Holy Spirit prompt me to read and speak life-giving words. In Your name, Amen.

Write a letter to your Heavenly Daddy telling Him what happens to you when you read His Word.

_____

_____

_____

_____

_____

_____

_____

_____

_____

_____

_____

_____

_____

_____

_____

_____

_____

_____

_____

_____

_____

~Day 117~

YOU DON'T NEED TO BEG ME FOR WHAT YOU ALREADY HAVE

I saw a vision of a man ordering a free package online. He saw something that said he was qualified to receive this package for free, so he ordered it. I saw the package from the beginning to the end. I saw it being loaded into different trucks. Each time it was loaded, it was a little more damaged. I saw the box get thrown around, stepped on, and the cardboard become worn and even shredded in some areas. Finally, I saw the package arrive at the man's house. The postal man rang the doorbell and gave the package to the man. He even logged the time and date as proof of confirmation that the job was "finished." The man brought the package into his house.

The next scene I saw was of this same man on the phone with the company he ordered the package from. He was talking to the man in charge and saying, "When am I going to receive my package? I need my package. Where is my package? I am entitled to this package. I am begging you, please send my package." The man in charge was puzzled. He said, "Sir, your package was already delivered. I even have proof of delivery. You already have it. You don't need to beg us for it. I suggest that you go and look for it, and you will find it." This man was distraught and full of anxiety trying to receive something he already had. Then I heard these words from the Lord:

"My precious children, oh, how I long for you to understand what is already yours! This vision symbolizes many of My children begging Me for a package they have already received. In the vision, the man ordering the package symbolizes you asking Me to be Lord of your life. When you did this, I freely came to live in you. I symbolize the box as I had a tiring journey to the cross after being beaten and ripped to shreds. I prevailed. I rose again the third day. When you asked Me into your life, you received Me as your beautiful package loaded with spiritual blessings. You already have every spiritual blessing including total forgiveness and healing and so much more. You are entitled to it. You qualify for it. The proof of delivery is My Word! It is all recorded in the Word. I would love you to search deep in the Word and see what is already yours. You will find it.

"Child, when you beg Me and beg Me to forgive you or heal you, it grieves Me. I am not withholding from you. I want you to discover what is already yours and receive it. Like the man in charge who symbolized Me in the vision, I tell you that it has already been delivered. I bought this package with My own blood. Receive it free of charge. You are entitled to it because it is a wonderful gift. Come boldly to My throne of grace and accept the package. Dig deep into the Word for more revelation, and I will surely give it to you. Are you hungry for this revelation? Are you desperate for this revelation? Do you want it with all of your heart? Are you tired of striving and begging and pleading? Beloved, let Me lovingly show you what belongs to you. It brings Me so much joy when My children dig deep and receive the revelations they hunger for.

"Child, I love you so much and am filled with so much compassion when you are struggling to receive what is freely yours. Come to Me, and I will comfort you and guide you. Don't ever give up hope. Come to Me. Let Me show you what you need to know. If you never hear that something belongs to you, you will not receive it. That is why I will continue to tell you what is already yours. I will continue to renew your mind with the truth. It is so you will be abundantly blessed. You cannot fathom My great love for you. It is so much more than you could ever imagine. With this incredible love, how could I not give you a wonderful package filled with blessings that contain everything you need? My love bought the package. It was delivered at the cross with love."

Ephesians 2:8; Psalm 103:1-5, 12; Ephesians 1:3-8; Hebrews 9:14; 10:19-22; Isaiah 53:5

There are so many more Scriptures. Let your deep hunger for this revelation prompt you to dig deeper to find them. Pray that Holy Spirit will show them to you.

Prayer:

Heavenly Daddy, I am in awe from this vision. It helps me to see that You long for me to receive everything that You have already given me because You love me so much and want to see me prosper in this life. Daddy, I hunger for more and more revelation of what is mine. It will take me a lifetime and eternity to discover all that You have done, yet, I never want to stop growing. Daddy, help me to go higher. Help me to discover more of Who You are. I vow to stop begging You for what I already have. Rather, I will start thanking You for finishing it all for me. In Your precious name, Amen.

*Spend some time digging in the Scriptures. Ask Daddy to speak to you and show you what is already yours. Keep thanking Him for the beautiful package He gave you free of charge.

Bless the Lord, O my soul, and forget not all His benefits"
- Psalm 103:2

After reviewing all the Scriptures on today's list, write down all the benefits of the Lord that come to your mind, including ones you didn't realize He had promised.

_____

_____

_____

_____

_____

_____

_____

_____

_____

_____

_____

_____

_____

_____

_____

_____

_____

_____

_____

~Day 118~

I AM SO MUCH BIGGER

I saw a vision of a demon tormenting a woman. He was feeding her all kinds of fear thoughts. I saw that she was in extreme fear and torment. Next, I saw Jesus take her to a mirror that opened her eyes into the spiritual realm. When she looked in the mirror, she saw how puny and tiny this little demon of fear was. She pointed at it and started laughing hysterically. The demon knew that he was exposed and his mission was finished. He left. Next, the woman saw herself in the mirror. She saw Jesus in her. Jesus was so huge that, even though He was inside her, He towered all the way to the heavens. She got a revelation of who she was in Him and said, "He who is in me is greater than he who is in the world" (1 John 4:4).

Next, I saw this same demon along with several others come back to the woman. The woman started hearing all kinds of fear-filled thoughts. She was also hearing thoughts of resentment, anger, and jealousy. Suddenly, she remembered who she was in Christ. She remembered that these thoughts were from another kingdom. She started laughing hysterically as she remembered how puny the demon was in the first vision and how huge Jesus was in her. The demon left again, and she was left praising Jesus. She again said, "He who is in me is greater than he who is in the world" (1 John 4:4). Then I heard these words:

"My dear children, I am so much bigger. I am so much greater. I have already won the battle for you and purchased your freedom from the kingdom of darkness. I live in you. All the power to overcome every single demonic thought, lie, and scheme lives in you. I want you to get a revelation of how powerless and pathetic that kingdom is so that you realize you no longer have to put up with its tactics. Take a stand and say, "No!" when they try to get you to participate with their evil thoughts. Or just laugh and laugh hysterically. Feel the joy when you laugh because I have given you total power over the enemy. Again, I tell you that the only power he has is the power you give him over your life.

"Beloved, when you start dwelling on thoughts that bring you down, I want you to take a stand against them and fill your mind with the truth. Fill your mind with whatever is right, whatever is true, whatever is holy and pure. The more you do this, the more freedom and joy you will experience. Start dwelling on My love for you. Start dwelling on the truths of who you are in Me. The more you dwell on these truths, the more power will be manifested in your daily life. You will be filled with faith because you will be believing truth instead of lies. Your mind will go from racing with negative thoughts to resting in the truth.

"I want you to realize Who lives in you. Do you really know that I live in you? I will remind you again that, because I live in you, you are filled with everything you need to live an abundant life filled with power. You are already filled with life, health, power, love, and so much more. Let this revelation rise up in you whenever you need to stand against the enemy who wants to continually steal, kill, and destroy you. Let it break out! I am so much bigger, and I live in you! Beloved, take your peace back and don't let the enemy steal it from you any longer."

1 John 4:4; Luke 10:19; Colossians 3:1-4; Romans 12:2; Philippians 4:8; Colossians 1:27

Prayer:

Heavenly Daddy, thank You for this reminder to continually think on things above. When the enemy comes in with thoughts to bring me down, remind me to take a stand against those lies. Father, I commit to dwelling on the truth that sets me free. I commit to dwelling on Your love for me. I commit to dwelling on holy thoughts. I commit to dwelling on who I am in You. I commit to dwelling on You living in me. I desire a deeper revelation of Christ in me, the hope of glory. Daddy, thank You for also reminding me that Your power lives in me and You have given me all the power I need to be able to stand against all tactics of the enemy. You are amazing. In Jesus' name, Amen.

*Commit to thinking only positive, Heavenly thoughts today, and, when the enemy tries to come in with negative, fear-filled thoughts, take a stand against him and start praising Jesus Who is not only way bigger, but Who loves you so much that He came to live in you.

Day 118 ~ I Am So Much Bigger

Write about how this vision effected you.

~Day 119~

JESUS' LOVE FOR THE ENTIRE WORLD

I saw a vision of Jesus. It was a very touching vision. I saw that He was pregnant. He was pregnant with the world, and I saw Him caressing His stomach ever so gently as a pregnant mother does to the child inside her. I heard Him say:

"I want every person in the world to realize how much I love them. I love the entire world. I came to save the entire world, yet not everyone will come into the Kingdom. This grieves Me very much. I want you to share the good news. I want you to share with everyone how much I love and adore every single person who was ever created. I love and adore everyone, every tribe, and every nation. I love them all with a passionate, burning love.

"As a mother takes care of and protects the child inside her, even more do I love, care for, and protect My people. You know how a mother is excited to see the child that she is carrying, the child that is part of her and created in her image, be born into the world? I am even more excited to see every person I created come into the world. I wanted every single person on the earth. Every person was created in My image, including you. I knew you before you were born. I was with you in the womb, and I rejoiced the day you were born. I love every single person in the world. I love the generations that have passed on, and I love the future generation waiting to come into the world. I love them all, saved and unsaved. They are all created in My image.

"Beloved, I want you to know that you are My child whom I adore. Even though I have many children to love on, I love spending alone time with you. Yes, I love spending one on one time with you. You are special and unique to Me. There will never be another just like you in the entire world. You were handpicked to be you, and I adore you just the way you are. Come, spend some time with Me, precious one. Let Me love on you and you alone."

John 3:16-17; Psalm 139; Genesis 1:26; Psalm 24:1

Prayer:

Jesus, thank You for coming to save me. Thank You for protecting me, caring for me, and loving me. Thank You for showing me the passionate love that You have for me. Help me to share this good news with others and bring more people into the Kingdom. It brings me joy that You enjoy spending alone time with just me. I am that special to You. That makes my heart skip a beat. I love You so much, my precious Savior. In Your name, Amen.

Do you see yourself as special to your Heavenly Daddy? Why or why not? If not, journal about it, break that lie over your life, and ask your Daddy to give you a revelation of how much He adores you.

~Day 120~

WILL YOU DANCE WITH ME?

"My bride, I see you discouraged. I see you sitting there listening to the voices of the enemy telling you that you have failed again, you are not worthy to be loved, and you will never see your breakthrough.

"Let Me show you what I see. I see you sitting there dressed in a bridal gown. I see a bride dressed in white, perfected by My holy blood. I see you as white as snow. I see a bride I was willing to die for. I see a bride I am longing to spend eternity with.

"Precious one, feel Me now. Feel My loving arms wrapped around you. Feel Me lift you up and ask you to dance with Me. Will you take My hand and let Me dance with My beautiful, perfect bride? It is in My arms that you will find breakthrough. It is in My arms that you will be encouraged by My love for you.

"Let's dance together! Let's laugh together. Let's have fun together, and let's watch the enemy flee together. He sees you are married to Me. He sees the joy you feel in My arms that he will never be able to feel. He wants to rob you of being My bride because he knows he will never be able to experience the love, joy, and peace I give to My own. Child, don't let the enemy rob you any longer. Stay with Me. Dance with Me. I long to love on you."

Isaiah 1:18; Romans 5:8; Song of Solomon 4:7

Prayer:

Jesus, I accept Your invitation to come dance with You. Take me in Your arms and love on me. Help me to see that, because of Your blood, I am washed white as snow. I choose to ignore the voice of the enemy that tells me lies in order to keep me in discouragement. Instead, I take the peace, joy, and love that You promised me. I pray that You even give me an image or a dream of us dancing together. In Jesus' name, Amen!

*Keep renewing your mind today by saying, "I am the bride of Christ. He is my lover. He chose me to be His forever. I am His beautiful bride, and He is my faithful husband forever and ever." Keep repeating this until you feel the joy come.

Journal about what it means to you to be Jesus' lover and bride.

_____
_____
_____
_____
_____
_____
_____
_____
_____
_____
_____
_____
_____
_____
_____
_____
_____
_____
_____
_____
_____
_____
_____
_____
_____
_____
_____

~Day 121~

YOU ARE FOREVER LOCKED INTO MY FAMILY AND MY LOVING ARMS

I saw a painful vision. I saw visions of different families. In some of the families, I saw the father leave. The rest of the family was left grieving and weeping. In some of the families, I saw the mother leave, and again the rest of the family was left grieving and weeping. I saw some families where the children were taken away. The parents and children were all hysterically screaming and weeping and devastated to be separated from one another. They would hold their arms out to each other, but I saw the children being taken away. I saw children who had been given up for adoption go to loving families, yet later on, I saw some of these children being ripped away from their adoptive parents. I saw some children trying to talk to a parent who was high on drugs, but they gave up, felt lonely and uncared for, and went to their rooms sobbing and longing for the love they were not receiving. I saw a lot of hurt and pain in this vision. I felt our Heavenly Daddy's heart of love and compassion for any child who has experienced any of these situations. I heard Him say this:

"My precious children, I tell you that the day you decided you wanted to be with Me is the day that locked you into My family and My loving arms forever. No one will ever be able to take you away from Me or separate you from My loving arms. No one. You are forever mine, and I will never, ever let you go. I am ALWAYS available to you, always, and you forever have My attention.

"My beautiful children, some of you have experienced the heartache and pain of an earthly parent abandoning you or of being ripped away from your parents. Some of you have even felt abandoned by a parent who was physically there with you as you grew up, yet emotionally unavailable due to addictions or mental illness. I have so much love and compassion for you. My heart broke when I saw what the enemy did to you and your family. I want you to know it was never My plan to have you go through such heartache, torment, and pain. You are My beloved child, and it grieves Me to see My children abandoned, abused, neglected, and in pain. Precious one, give it all to Me. Give Me your pain. Give Me your hurt. Give Me your fear of abandonment. Give Me your fear of rejection. Give Me the wounds and let Me heal them. Let Me fill the void that has been missing your whole life. Let Me fill it. Let Me break off the lie that says that I am not there for you when you need Me. Let Me break the lie that says that you are not important enough to Me. Those are lies. Let Me replace all lies with the truth that will set you free.

Day 121 ~ You Are Forever Locked Into My Family and My Loving Arms

"You were created to be My child. You were created to be in My loving arms for all eternity. Child, do not fear that I will ever leave you. I will never leave you. I will never stop wrapping My arms around you. I will never stop being your Daddy. Child, I want you to realize with your whole heart that you are forever mine and forever in My embrace. You are special to Me. There is a special place just for you in My arms and no one else can fill that place created just for you. Beloved, you are so special to Me. Let it sink in that nothing will ever separate you from Me or My love for you, nothing. You are locked into My Kingdom family forever and ever, and I am so filled with joy when I think about us being together for all eternity.

"Child, come to Me. If you are feeling pain, bring it to Daddy now. Let Me love on you. Let Me kiss your wounds with My love. Let Me remind you that you are safe now. You are safe with your Daddy, and no one will take you from Me because you are forever locked into My loving arms. No failure can ever separate you from My embrace. Nothing can remove the grip I have on you.

"Precious child of Mine, let Me speak to you and show you that I have always been with you. Let Me love on you right now and do some inner healing in your life. I want to see you set free. I want to see you transformed. There is no wound too big for Me to heal. Let Me heal you now, My beloved."

Romans 8:38-39; Psalm 34:18; John 10:29; Psalm 147:3

Prayer:

Heavenly Father, thank You for forever being my Daddy. You are so precious to me. Daddy, I still have a wound that came in during my childhood. I pray that You would heal all of the wounds that came in with abandonment, abuse, and neglect. Heavenly Daddy, You know what needs to be healed and kissed with Your love. As I come into the secret place, I pray that You would speak to me and show me the wounds that need to be healed. I pray that You would show me that You were always with me, even when I didn't sense Your presence. Show me some things from the past through Your eyes so that I can let them go, forgive people, and be completely healed, which is my inheritance. Thank You for taking care of my every need. In Jesus' name, Amen.

Journal about what this vision means to you.

~Day 122~

MY LOVE ABOVE ALL ELSE

I saw a vision of Jesus in Heaven. He had a megaphone and pointed it towards the earth. He said, "I love you, I love you, I love you." Then, I saw families watching television, and Jesus appeared on the screen and said, "I love you. Do you know how much I love you? Do you know that I am the answer to all of the problems you are going through?"

Then, I saw Jesus appear at some self-help meetings. He said, "You need to know how much I love you. That is what will help you. This is the answer you have been searching for." Next, I saw Jesus appear in recovery meetings. He said, "I am the way to complete and total healing. Come, let Me show you how much I love you. Let Me fill you with My love so that you never, ever want to go back to the enemy's counterfeit love."

Then, I saw Jesus appear in some churches. I saw pastors, priests, and teachers preaching condemnation and shame. Jesus stopped them and said, "No, they need to know My love for them. They need to know My love above all else. My love is what holds the universe together. My love is why you are even here on the earth. Knowing My love is the only way My people will be able to live a holy life by the Spirit. They need to know My love."

Next, I saw Jesus go out on the streets to a drug-infested neighborhood. He was pointing to the drug addicts and saying, "They need to know My love. Where are My people? Why are they staying in the churches and not going out into the world? Where are My people? Go and tell these broken, hopeless people how much I love them."

Next, I saw Jesus in a big city. There were homeless people lying on the ground with signs asking for money. I saw Jesus lifting one of their heads up in His hands, and He said these words to me:

"This man needs to know how much I love him. He needs to know that I have set him free. Who will tell him? I want the world to know My love above all else. Will you help Me?

"Beloved, do you know My love for you? Do you really know My love for you? Precious one, it is the key to all your needs. It is the key to experiencing Me. Will you help Me share My love with the world? Will you help Me? The world needs to know what I did for them. They need to know that I already purchased their salvation, healing, prosperity, freedom, and so much more. They need to know that I took all of their sins, sorrows, and pain on the cross. They need to know it. They need to know that I did all of this because of My great love for them. I desire the entire world to come and be with Me forever basking in My love, yet I know many don't make it. I grieve for the lost ones. I grieve for them. I love every human whom I created. I love them all. Will you help Me to share My love with the world?"

Mark 16:15; John 3:16; Isaiah 53; Jeremiah 31:3; John 14:12

Prayer:

Yes, Jesus, I will go and tell the world the good news that You are the way, the truth, and the life. Show me where to go, and I will tell the world of Your love. I say, "Yes Lord." Let my actions show Your love to the lost. I want to spread the news that You are so good. In Your name, Amen.

*Think about a way you can share the love of Christ with broken, hurting, lost people. Pray and see where Daddy leads you. When you share His love with others, He is so very touched.

Journal about how this vision touched you personally.

_____
_____
_____
_____
_____
_____
_____
_____
_____
_____
_____
_____
_____
_____
_____
_____
_____
_____
_____
_____

SALVATION PRAYER

Romans 10:9 (NLT) - "If you confess with your mouth that Jesus is Lord and you believe in your heart that God raised Him from the dead, you will be saved."

If you have never accepted Jesus as your Lord and Savior and you would like to do so, all you need to do is simply believe and receive. Repeat the following prayer from your heart:

"Jesus, I confess with my mouth that You are my Lord and Savior. I believe in my heart that my Heavenly Father raised You from the dead. Thank You for taking away my sins on the cross. I receive the forgiveness that You purchased for me right now. Thank You for coming to live in me this very moment. I look forward to spending eternity with You. Help me to get to know You intimately. I pray that I would know and experience the passionate, burning love You have for me for all eternity. Please give me a hunger to read Your Word so that I continue to grow spiritually. Thank You for saving me! In Your precious name, Amen!"

Welcome to the Kingdom of Heaven. You are Daddy's precious child forever. The angels are rejoicing at this very moment because you will spend eternity forever in Heaven.

BAPTISM IN THE HOLY SPIRIT PRAYER

If you desire to receive your inheritance of supernatural power, all you have to do is ask and believe that you have it. Luke 11:10-13 says that if you ask, you will receive. It says that Heavenly Father loves to give you good gifts, including the gift of Holy Spirit. Pray the following prayer:

"Heavenly Daddy, I need the power of Holy Spirit to live the Christian life. Please fill me with Your precious Holy Spirit right now. I receive this special gift as part of my inheritance from You because You love to give Your children good gifts. Thank You for baptizing me at this very moment."

Open your mouth in faith and speak any words that rise up in you. Tongues is one of Daddy's love gifts to you. Try to speak in tongues whenever you can, and you will truly be blessed.

ABOUT THE AUTHOR

Nichole Marbach resides in Illinois with her husband, three children, and three shelties. She enjoys prophesying Heavenly Father's heart of love to His children so they can be healed, praying for broken and hurting people, and giving her testimony in which she gives Jesus all the glory for setting her free. She carries a deep understanding of the finished work of Christ wherever she goes and longs to see the Body of Christ receive the revelation that the cross changed everything. She also desires to see God's children receive the full inheritance that Jesus purchased in order to experience the abundant life, and delights in talking about the goodness of God and how He longs for and deeply desires a close, intimate relationship with all of His children. Her personal testimony of overcoming many mental illnesses, including bipolar disorder, suicide attempts, self-injury, hospitalizations, alcoholism and other addictions has given her a passion to help others embrace Jesus and the cross (1 Corinthians 2:2) in order to walk in freedom, wholeness, and overflowing joy.

**For more information about this book
or how to contact Nichole visit:**

**www.NicholeMarbach.com
www.comeandreceive.com**

Additional copies of this book
and other book titles from
XP Media and XP Publishing
are available at **XPmedia.com**

BULK ORDERS:

We have bulk/wholesale prices for stores and ministries. Please contact: usaresource@xpmedia.com.

For Canadian bulk orders please contact:
resource@xpmedia.com

CSA
PUBLISHING

www.XPpublishing.com
A Ministry of Patricia King and
Christian Services Association

272